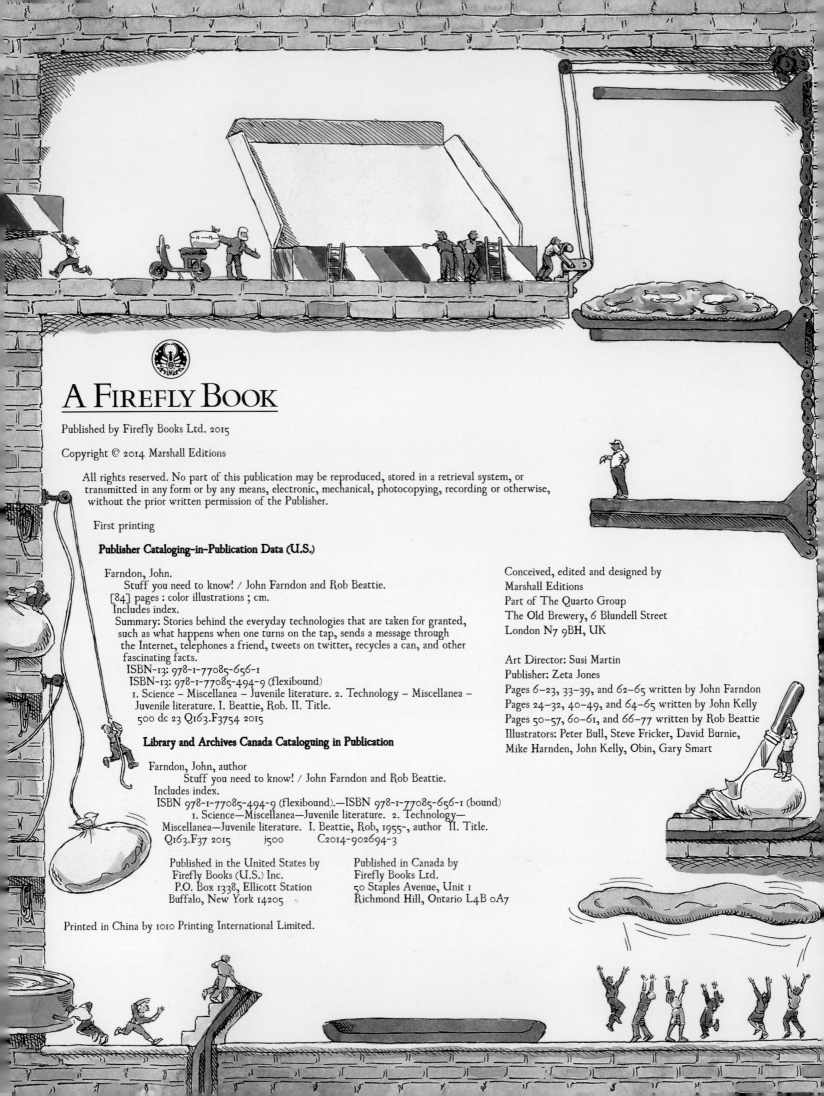

A FIREFLY BOOK

Published by Firefly Books Ltd. 2015

First printing

Publisher Cataloging-in-Publication Data (U.S.)

Farndon, John.
    Stuff you need to know! / John Farndon and Rob Beattie.
    [84] pages : color illustrations ; cm.
    Includes index.
    Summary: Stories behind the everyday technologies that are taken for granted, such as what happens when one turns on the tap, sends a message through the Internet, telephones a friend, tweets on twitter, recycles a can, and other fascinating facts.
    ISBN-13: 978-1-77085-656-1
    ISBN-13: 978-1-77085-494-9 (flexibound)
    1. Science – Miscellanea – Juvenile literature. 2. Technology – Miscellanea – Juvenile literature. I. Beattie, Rob. II. Title.
    500 dc 23 Q163.F3754 2015

Library and Archives Canada Cataloguing in Publication

Farndon, John, author
    Stuff you need to know! / John Farndon and Rob Beattie.
    Includes index.
    ISBN 978-1-77085-494-9 (flexibound).—ISBN 978-1-77085-656-1 (bound)
    1. Science—Miscellanea—Juvenile literature. 2. Technology—Miscellanea—Juvenile literature. I. Beattie, Rob, 1955-, author II. Title.
    Q163.F37 2015   j500   C2014-902694-3

Published in the United States by
Firefly Books (U.S.) Inc.
P.O. Box 1338, Ellicott Station
Buffalo, New York 14205

Published in Canada by
Firefly Books Ltd.
50 Staples Avenue, Unit 1
Richmond Hill, Ontario L4B 0A7

Printed in China by 1010 Printing International Limited.

Conceived, edited and designed by
Marshall Editions
Part of The Quarto Group
The Old Brewery, 6 Blundell Street
London N7 9BH, UK

Art Director: Susi Martin
Publisher: Zeta Jones
Pages 6–23, 33–39, and 62–65 written by John Farndon
Pages 24–32, 40–49, and 64–65 written by John Kelly
Pages 50–57, 60–61, and 66–77 written by Rob Beattie
Illustrators: Peter Bull, Steve Fricker, David Burnie, Mike Harnden, John Kelly, Obin, Gary Smart

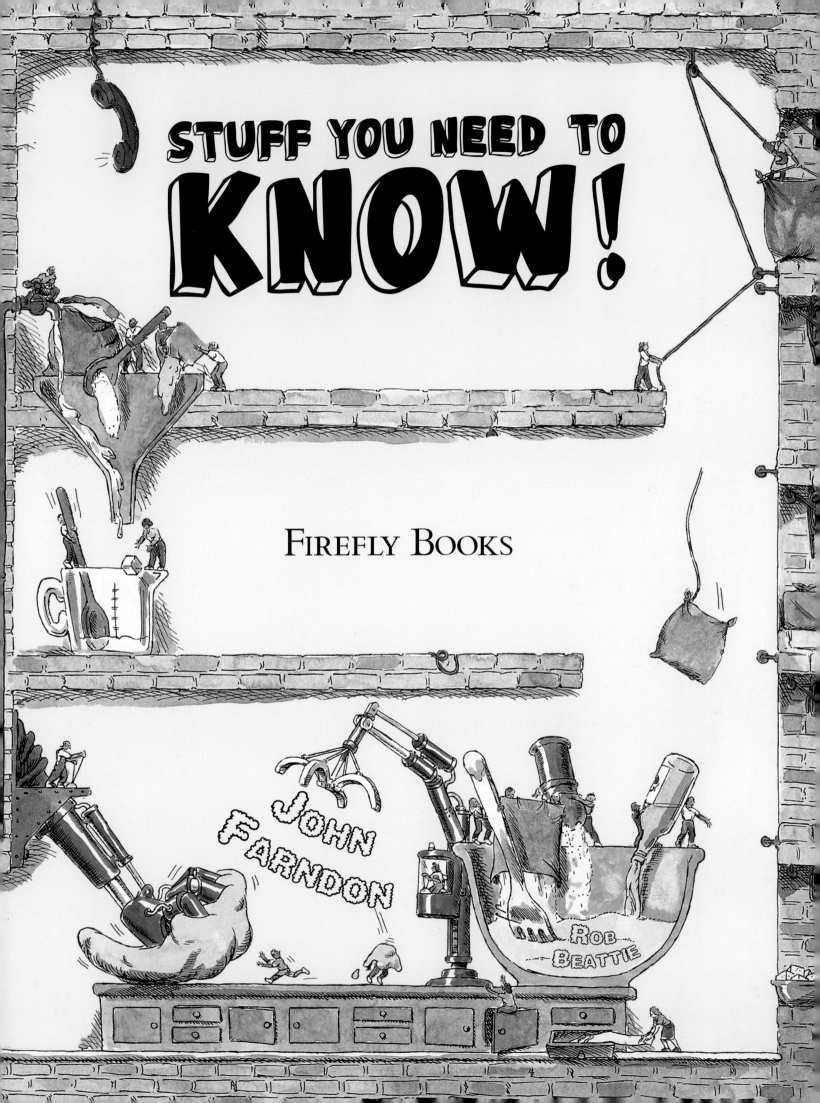

CONTENTS

* INDICATES A GATEFOLD SECTION

INTRODUCTION

Two hundred years ago, if you wanted light, water or food in your home, you had to go get it and carry it in yourself — unless you had servants to fetch it for you! Nowadays, you just flick a switch for light, turn on a faucet for water and pick up a phone to get food delivered. It all seems so easy!

In this house, you can see some of the things that we often take for granted in our homes. But just how do they work? That's what the little people in this book will show you.

Words that need further explanation are in **bold** and can be found on pages 78-79.

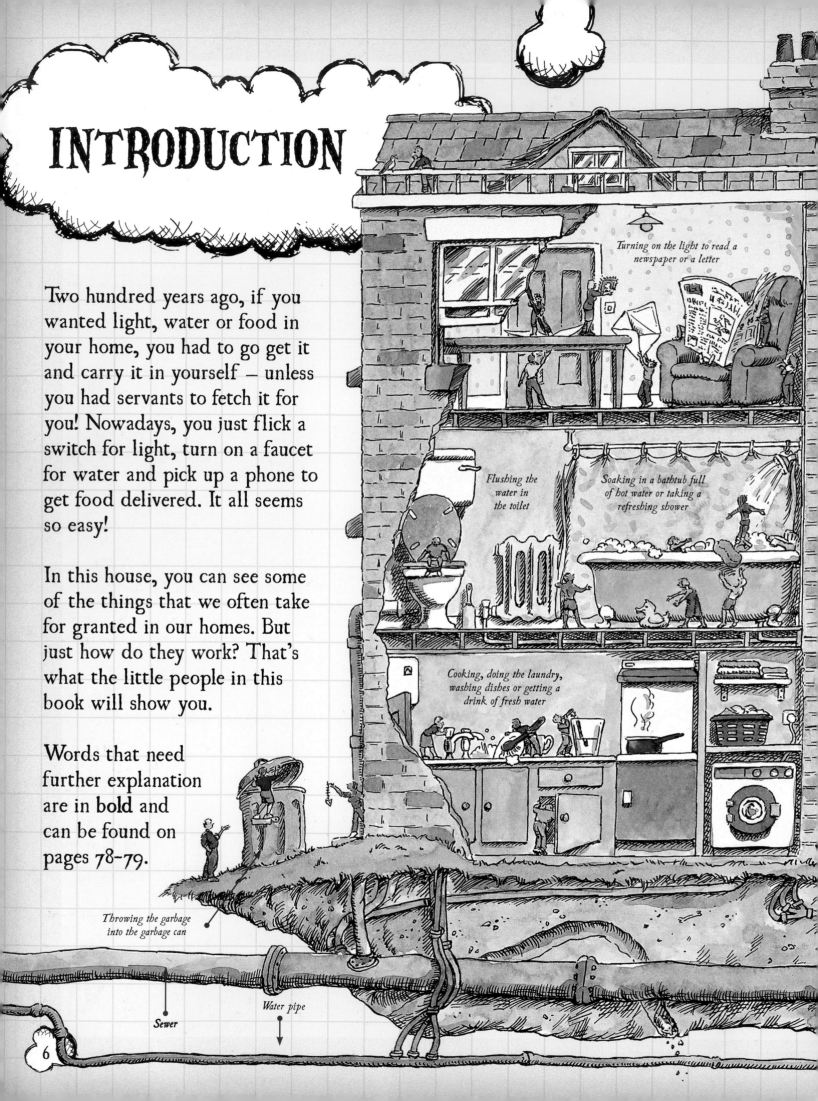

Turning on the light to read a newspaper or a letter

Flushing the water in the toilet

Soaking in a bathtub full of hot water or taking a refreshing shower

Cooking, doing the laundry, washing dishes or getting a drink of fresh water

Throwing the garbage into the garbage can

Sewer

Water pipe

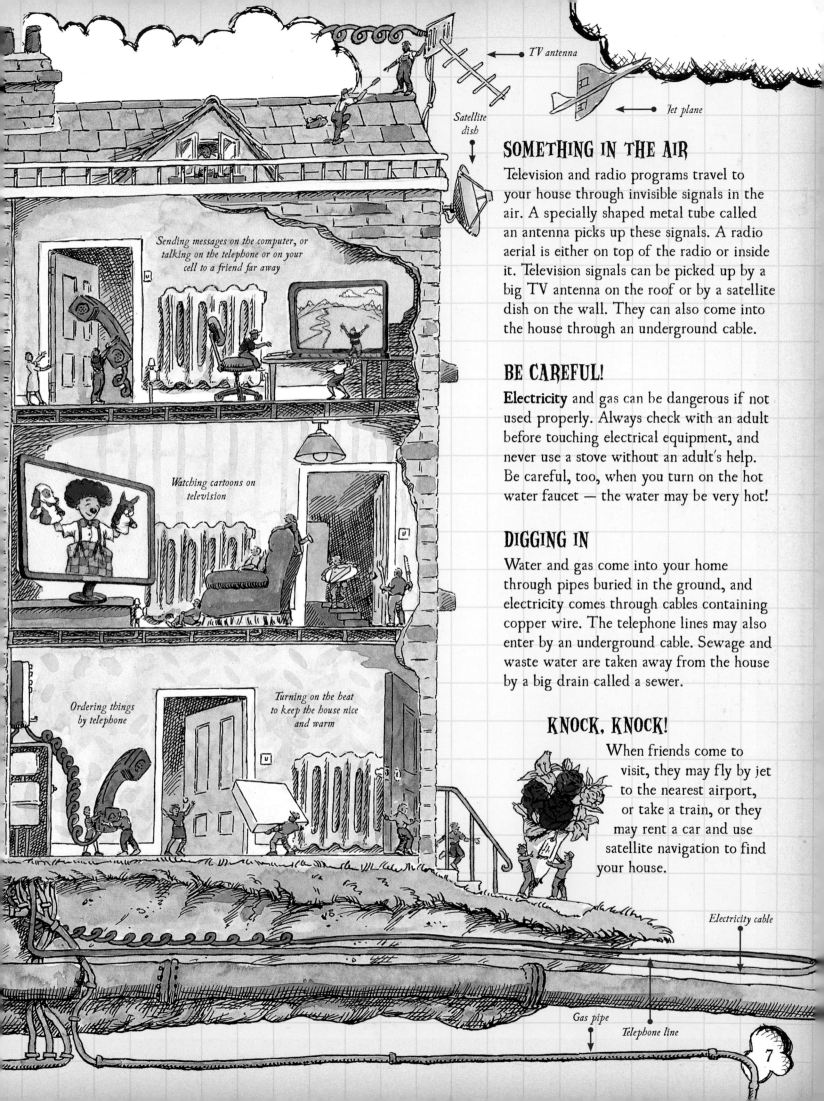

SOMETHING IN THE AIR

Television and radio programs travel to your house through invisible signals in the air. A specially shaped metal tube called an antenna picks up these signals. A radio aerial is either on top of the radio or inside it. Television signals can be picked up by a big TV antenna on the roof or by a satellite dish on the wall. They can also come into the house through an underground cable.

BE CAREFUL!

Electricity and gas can be dangerous if not used properly. Always check with an adult before touching electrical equipment, and never use a stove without an adult's help. Be careful, too, when you turn on the hot water faucet — the water may be very hot!

DIGGING IN

Water and gas come into your home through pipes buried in the ground, and electricity comes through cables containing copper wire. The telephone lines may also enter by an underground cable. Sewage and waste water are taken away from the house by a big drain called a sewer.

KNOCK, KNOCK!

When friends come to visit, they may fly by jet to the nearest airport, or take a train, or they may rent a car and use satellite navigation to find your house.

ELECTRICITY

When you turn on a lamp, an amazing invisible energy called electricity makes the lamp glow with light. Electricity is made, or generated, in a power plant. But how does it get from the power plant to the lamp in your house?

Hydroelectric power

Coal, oil, and gas power

Nuclear power

1 GETTING TO STEAM

Power plants burn coal, oil, gas or **nuclear fuel** to boil water into steam. The steam rushes along pipes and hits the blades of a wheel called a **turbine**, whirling it around quickly. In **hydroelectric stations**, water rushing down from a dam spins the turbine.

Rushing water   *Jet of steam*

2 GOING FOR A SPIN

As the turbine spins, it turns a coil of copper wire between the poles of a huge **magnet**. This is a **generator**.

Turbine blades spin around at high speed

The shaft of the turbine is linked to a generator

Magnet

Coil of copper wire

3 MAKING CURRENTS

The magnet's power drags tiny energy bundles, called **electrons**, through the wire. The electrons form a flow of electricity called an electric **current**.

Step-up transformer

4 RAISING THE CURRENT

The current from the power plant is too weak to reach your house. Its strength is raised, or stepped up, by sending it through an iron ring called a **transformer**.

A big wire picks up the electricity from the coil

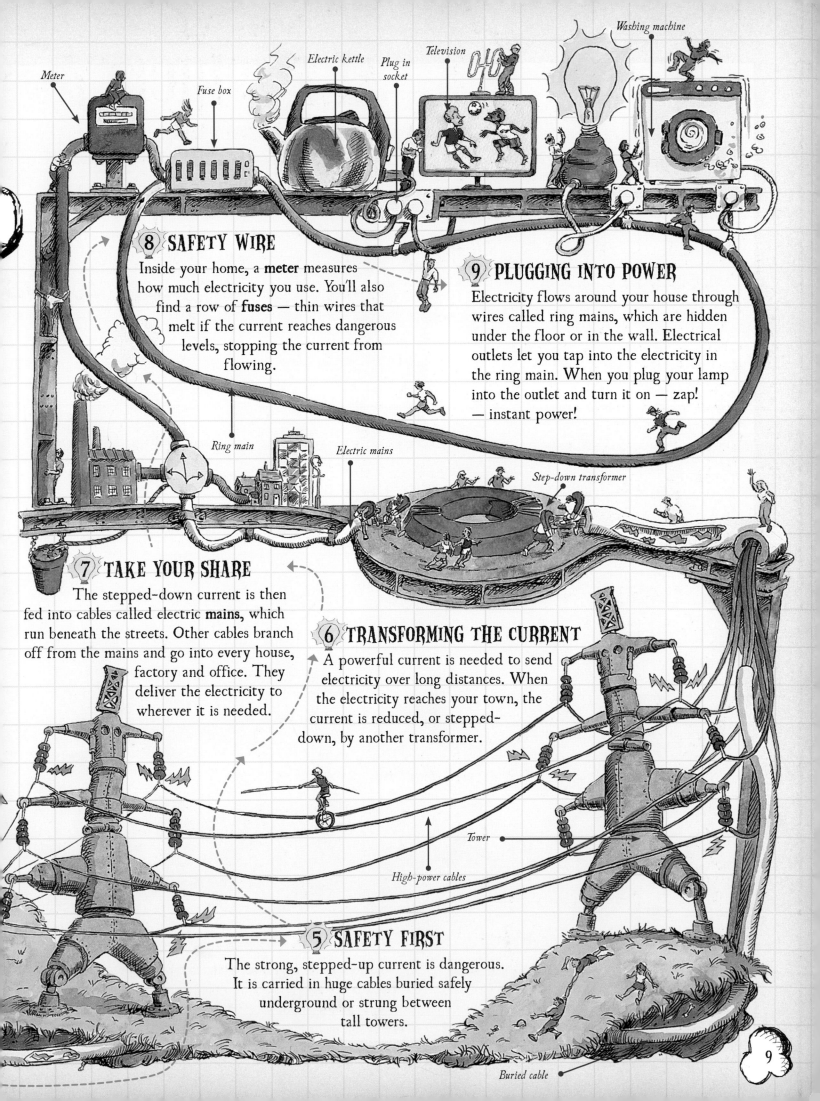

Meter

Fuse box

Electric kettle

Plug in socket

Television

Washing machine

8 SAFETY WIRE

Inside your home, a **meter** measures how much electricity you use. You'll also find a row of **fuses** — thin wires that melt if the current reaches dangerous levels, stopping the current from flowing.

9 PLUGGING INTO POWER

Electricity flows around your house through wires called ring mains, which are hidden under the floor or in the wall. Electrical outlets let you tap into the electricity in the ring main. When you plug your lamp into the outlet and turn it on — zap! — instant power!

Ring main

Electric mains

Step-down transformer

7 TAKE YOUR SHARE

The stepped-down current is then fed into cables called electric **mains,** which run beneath the streets. Other cables branch off from the mains and go into every house, factory and office. They deliver the electricity to wherever it is needed.

6 TRANSFORMING THE CURRENT

A powerful current is needed to send electricity over long distances. When the electricity reaches your town, the current is reduced, or stepped-down, by another transformer.

Tower

High-power cables

5 SAFETY FIRST

The strong, stepped-up current is dangerous. It is carried in huge cables buried safely underground or strung between tall towers.

Buried cable

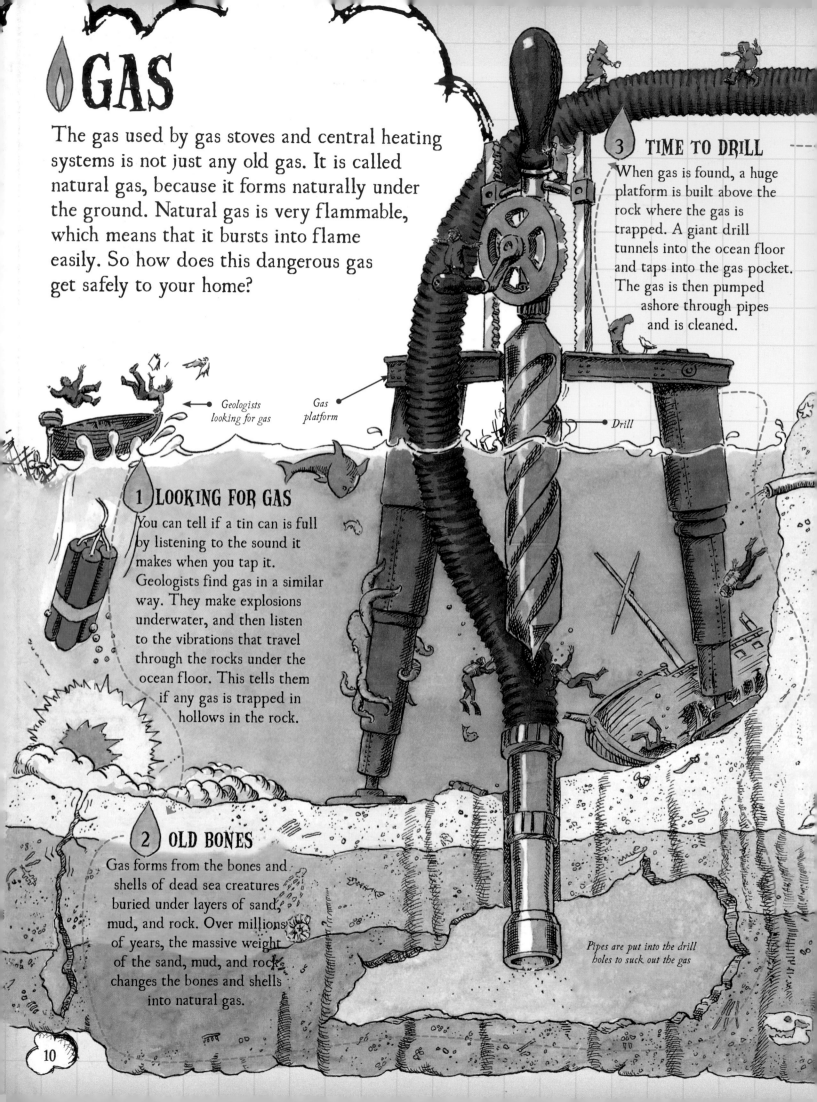

GAS

The gas used by gas stoves and central heating systems is not just any old gas. It is called natural gas, because it forms naturally under the ground. Natural gas is very flammable, which means that it bursts into flame easily. So how does this dangerous gas get safely to your home?

Geologists looking for gas

Gas platform

Drill

1 LOOKING FOR GAS

You can tell if a tin can is full by listening to the sound it makes when you tap it. Geologists find gas in a similar way. They make explosions underwater, and then listen to the vibrations that travel through the rocks under the ocean floor. This tells them if any gas is trapped in hollows in the rock.

2 OLD BONES

Gas forms from the bones and shells of dead sea creatures buried under layers of sand, mud, and rock. Over millions of years, the massive weight of the sand, mud, and rock changes the bones and shells into natural gas.

3 TIME TO DRILL

When gas is found, a huge platform is built above the rock where the gas is trapped. A giant drill tunnels into the ocean floor and taps into the gas pocket. The gas is then pumped ashore through pipes and is cleaned.

Pipes are put into the drill holes to suck out the gas

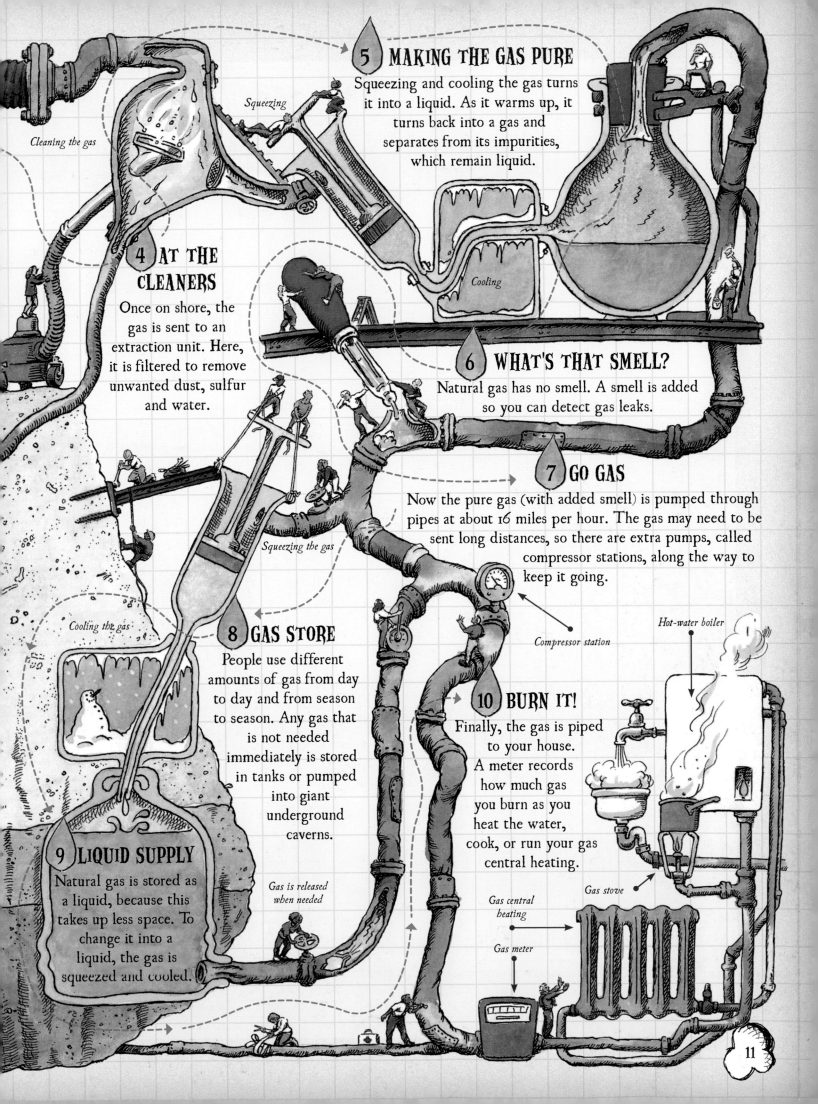

5 MAKING THE GAS PURE

Squeezing and cooling the gas turns it into a liquid. As it warms up, it turns back into a gas and separates from its impurities, which remain liquid.

Squeezing

Cleaning the gas

Cooling

4 AT THE CLEANERS

Once on shore, the gas is sent to an extraction unit. Here, it is filtered to remove unwanted dust, sulfur and water.

6 WHAT'S THAT SMELL?

Natural gas has no smell. A smell is added so you can detect gas leaks.

7 GO GAS

Now the pure gas (with added smell) is pumped through pipes at about 16 miles per hour. The gas may need to be sent long distances, so there are extra pumps, called compressor stations, along the way to keep it going.

Squeezing the gas

Cooling the gas

Compressor station

Hot-water boiler

8 GAS STORE

People use different amounts of gas from day to day and from season to season. Any gas that is not needed immediately is stored in tanks or pumped into giant underground caverns.

10 BURN IT!

Finally, the gas is piped to your house. A meter records how much gas you burn as you heat the water, cook, or run your gas central heating.

9 LIQUID SUPPLY

Natural gas is stored as a liquid, because this takes up less space. To change it into a liquid, the gas is squeezed and cooled.

Gas is released when needed

Gas central heating

Gas meter

Gas stove

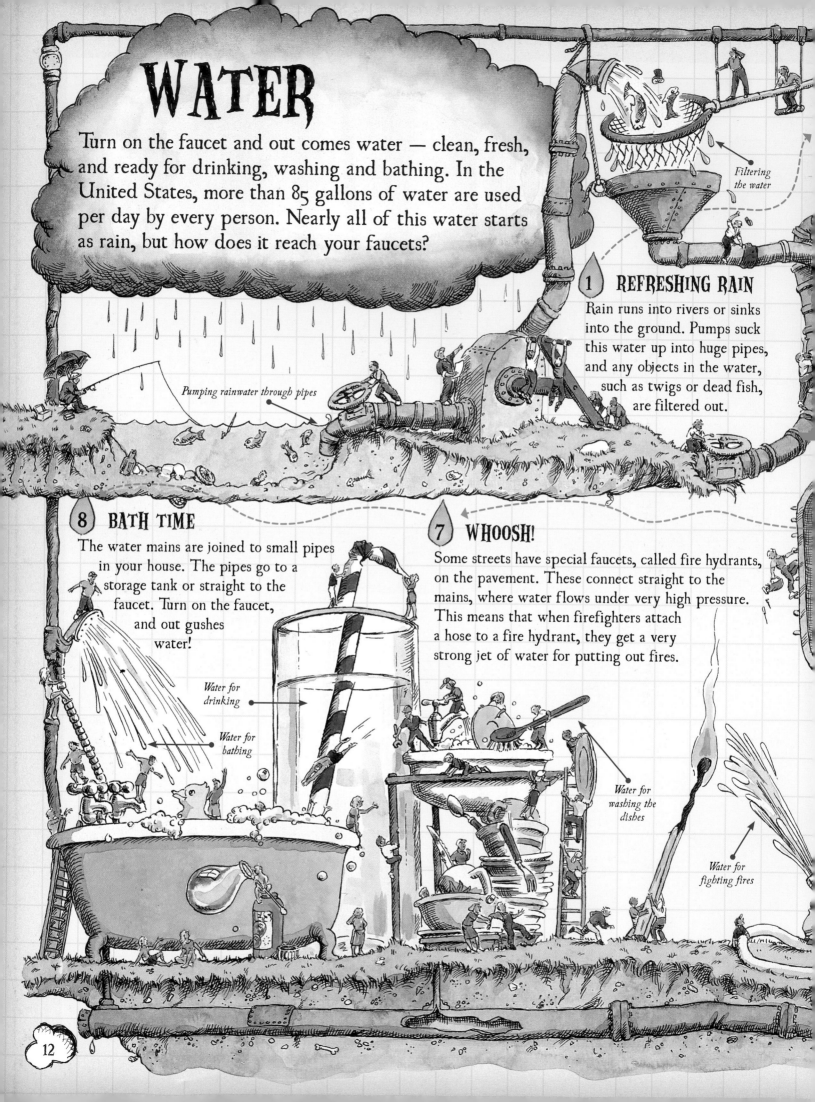

WATER

Turn on the faucet and out comes water — clean, fresh, and ready for drinking, washing and bathing. In the United States, more than 85 gallons of water are used per day by every person. Nearly all of this water starts as rain, but how does it reach your faucets?

Filtering the water

1 REFRESHING RAIN

Rain runs into rivers or sinks into the ground. Pumps suck this water up into huge pipes, and any objects in the water, such as twigs or dead fish, are filtered out.

Pumping rainwater through pipes

8 BATH TIME

The water mains are joined to small pipes in your house. The pipes go to a storage tank or straight to the faucet. Turn on the faucet, and out gushes water!

Water for drinking

Water for bathing

7 WHOOSH!

Some streets have special faucets, called fire hydrants, on the pavement. These connect straight to the mains, where water flows under very high pressure. This means that when firefighters attach a hose to a fire hydrant, they get a very strong jet of water for putting out fires.

Water for washing the dishes

Water for fighting fires

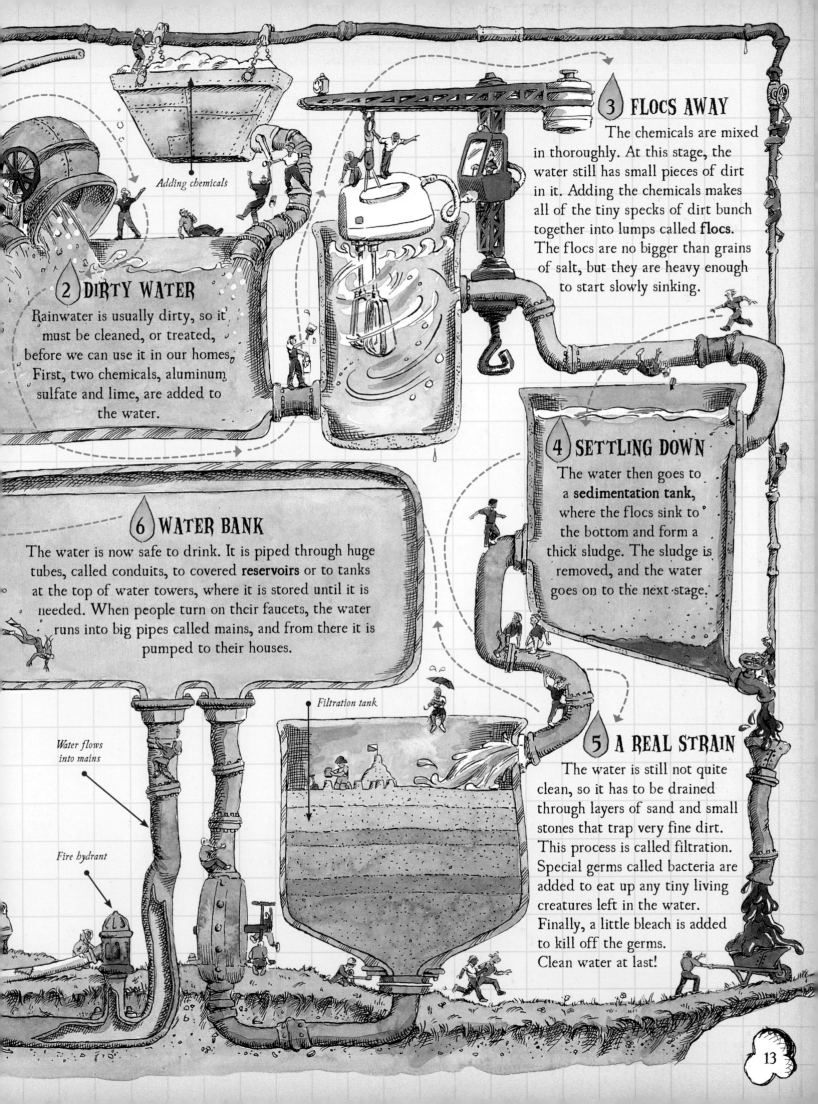

3 FLOCS AWAY

The chemicals are mixed in thoroughly. At this stage, the water still has small pieces of dirt in it. Adding the chemicals makes all of the tiny specks of dirt bunch together into lumps called **flocs**. The flocs are no bigger than grains of salt, but they are heavy enough to start slowly sinking.

Adding chemicals

2 DIRTY WATER

Rainwater is usually dirty, so it must be cleaned, or treated, before we can use it in our homes. First, two chemicals, aluminum sulfate and lime, are added to the water.

4 SETTLING DOWN

The water then goes to a **sedimentation tank**, where the flocs sink to the bottom and form a thick sludge. The sludge is removed, and the water goes on to the next stage.

6 WATER BANK

The water is now safe to drink. It is piped through huge tubes, called conduits, to covered **reservoirs** or to tanks at the top of water towers, where it is stored until it is needed. When people turn on their faucets, the water runs into big pipes called mains, and from there it is pumped to their houses.

Filtration tank

Water flows into mains

Fire hydrant

5 A REAL STRAIN

The water is still not quite clean, so it has to be drained through layers of sand and small stones that trap very fine dirt. This process is called filtration. Special germs called bacteria are added to eat up any tiny living creatures left in the water. Finally, a little bleach is added to kill off the germs. Clean water at last!

13

SEWAGE

When you pull the plug in the bath or flush the toilet, all the water and waste goes down the drain. But where does it go from there, and why doesn't the world just get smellier and smellier?

Away it goes!

6 THE FILTER BEDS

The dirty water is sprinkled onto the **filter beds**, which are made up of layers of slimy stones.

Filter beds

Steam from the boiling water powers the pumps in the sewage treatment plant

Methane from the sludge is burned to boil water

7 HELPFUL GERMS

The slime on the stones contains **bacteria**. These eat up any harmful material left in the water as it trickles down through the layers of stones.

Sludge digestion tank

Clean sludge from the digestion tank may be used as fertilizer

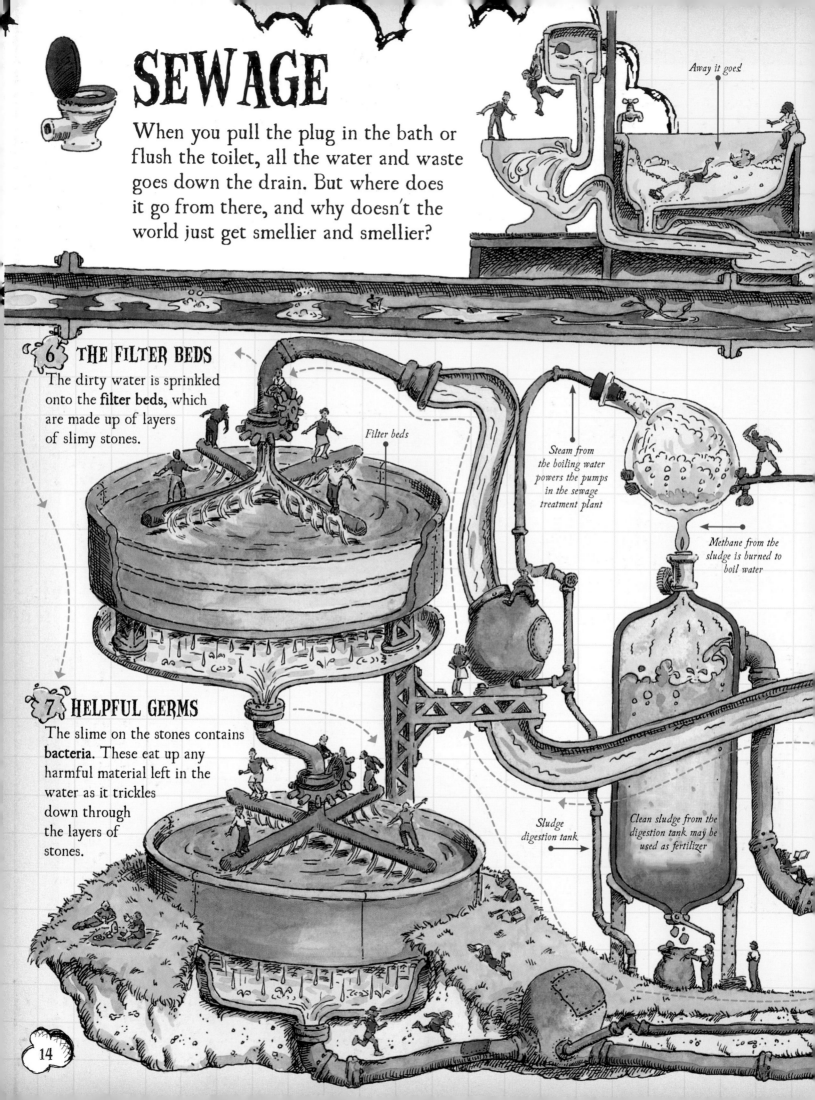

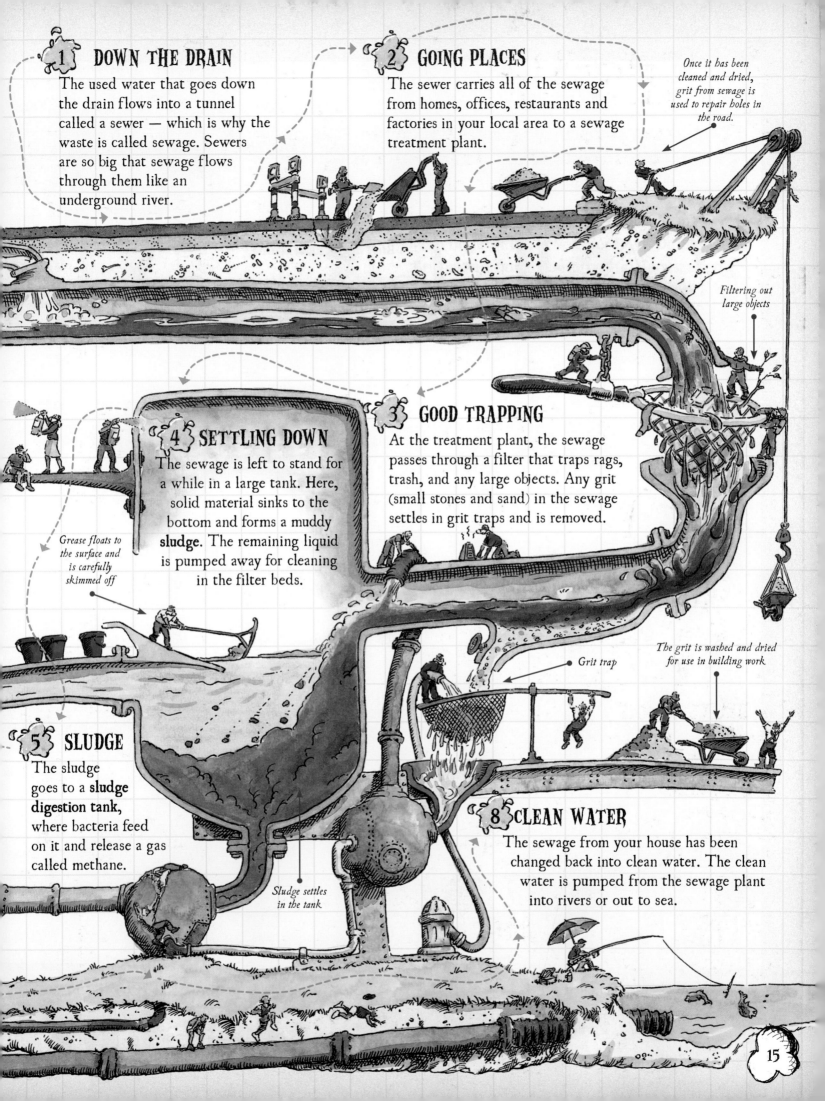

1 DOWN THE DRAIN

The used water that goes down the drain flows into a tunnel called a sewer — which is why the waste is called sewage. Sewers are so big that sewage flows through them like an underground river.

2 GOING PLACES

The sewer carries all of the sewage from homes, offices, restaurants and factories in your local area to a sewage treatment plant.

Once it has been cleaned and dried, grit from sewage is used to repair holes in the road.

Filtering out large objects

3 GOOD TRAPPING

At the treatment plant, the sewage passes through a filter that traps rags, trash, and any large objects. Any grit (small stones and sand) in the sewage settles in grit traps and is removed.

4 SETTLING DOWN

The sewage is left to stand for a while in a large tank. Here, solid material sinks to the bottom and forms a muddy **sludge**. The remaining liquid is pumped away for cleaning in the filter beds.

Grease floats to the surface and is carefully skimmed off

The grit is washed and dried for use in building work

Grit trap

5 SLUDGE

The sludge goes to a **sludge digestion tank,** where bacteria feed on it and release a gas called methane.

Sludge settles in the tank

8 CLEAN WATER

The sewage from your house has been changed back into clean water. The clean water is pumped from the sewage plant into rivers or out to sea.

15

TRASH

When you take out the trash, do you ever wonder what happens to it? Some things can be **recycled** and used again, but others have to be buried or burned.

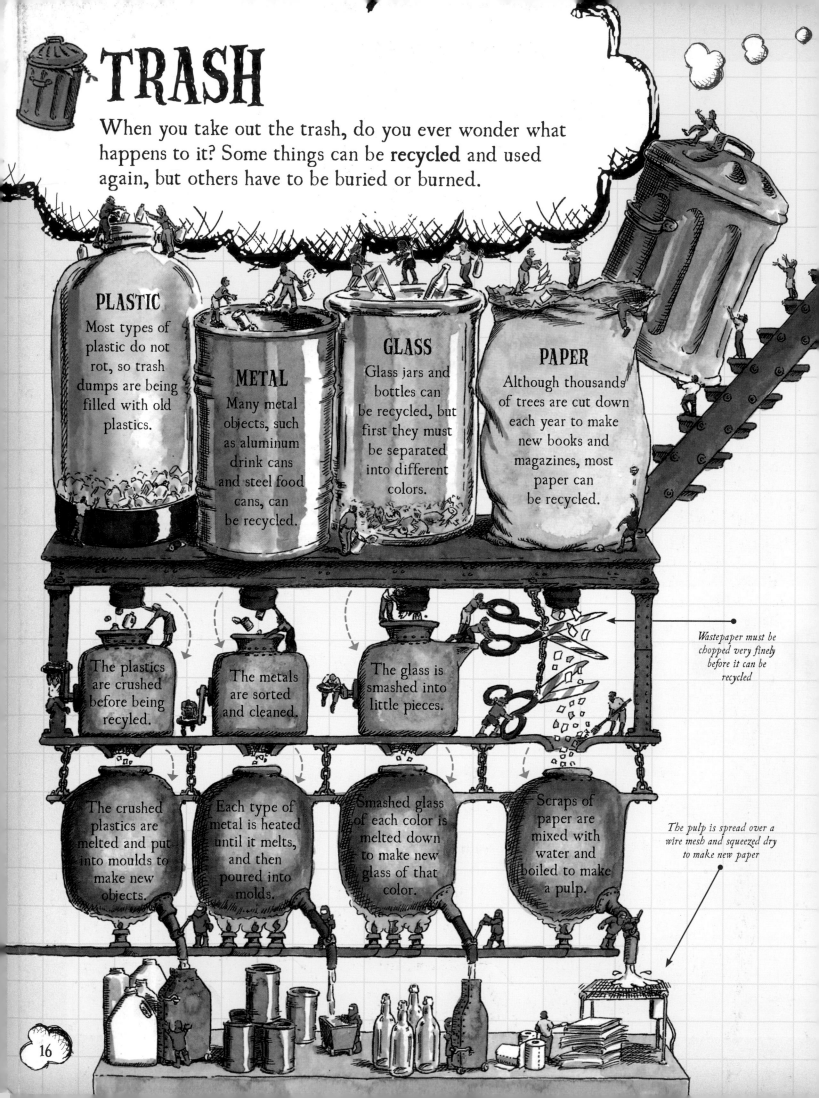

PLASTIC
Most types of plastic do not rot, so trash dumps are being filled with old plastics.

METAL
Many metal objects, such as aluminum drink cans and steel food cans, can be recycled.

GLASS
Glass jars and bottles can be recycled, but first they must be separated into different colors.

PAPER
Although thousands of trees are cut down each year to make new books and magazines, most paper can be recycled.

The plastics are crushed before being recyled.

The metals are sorted and cleaned.

The glass is smashed into little pieces.

Wastepaper must be chopped very finely before it can be recycled

The crushed plastics are melted and put into moulds to make new objects.

Each type of metal is heated until it melts, and then poured into molds.

Smashed glass of each color is melted down to make new glass of that color.

Scraps of paper are mixed with water and boiled to make a pulp.

The pulp is spread over a wire mesh and squeezed dry to make new paper

1 COLLECTING TRASH

Garbage trucks collect any trash that can't be recycled. They take it to garbage dumps or to **incinerators** to be burned.

4 NEW LAND

When the hole is full, the site is covered over. Once all the dangerous gases have been removed, the site can be used for something else.

2 AT THE DUMP

The trash is crushed to make it as small as possible. Then it is dumped into huge holes or pits in the ground called landfill sites.

Unloading the trash

Each layer of trash is covered with a layer of soil

3 HUGE PILE-UP

After being dumped in a hole, the crushed trash is packed down tight. As it rots, it gives off explosive gases that can be dangerous if it is allowed to build up. Pipes are built next to the hole so the gases can be collected or burned off.

SENDING MAIL

When you send a letter from New York City, in the United States, to Sydney, Australia, it somehow manages to find its way to the right address. Lift these pages to find out what happens.

THE RIGHT ADDRESS

Your letter won't reach its destination without the right address and **postal code** on the envelope. Each section of a street has a postal code — a sequence of letters and numbers. These help machines to sort the letters so they go to the right places.

HOW DOES THIS LETTER FROM THE USA GET TO

If you don't have any relatives or friends living abroad, ask your parents or teacher to help you find a pen pal overseas.

If you're writing to a friend, you may end your letter with "from" or "love from," and then your name.

If you're writing a business letter, you may end it with "Yours sincerely," and then your full name.

Put your own address at the top of the letter so that the person you're writing to knows where to send the reply. Include the date, too.

If you're writing to a fri[end], you may begin your le[tter] with "Dear," and the[n] friend's name.

18

20

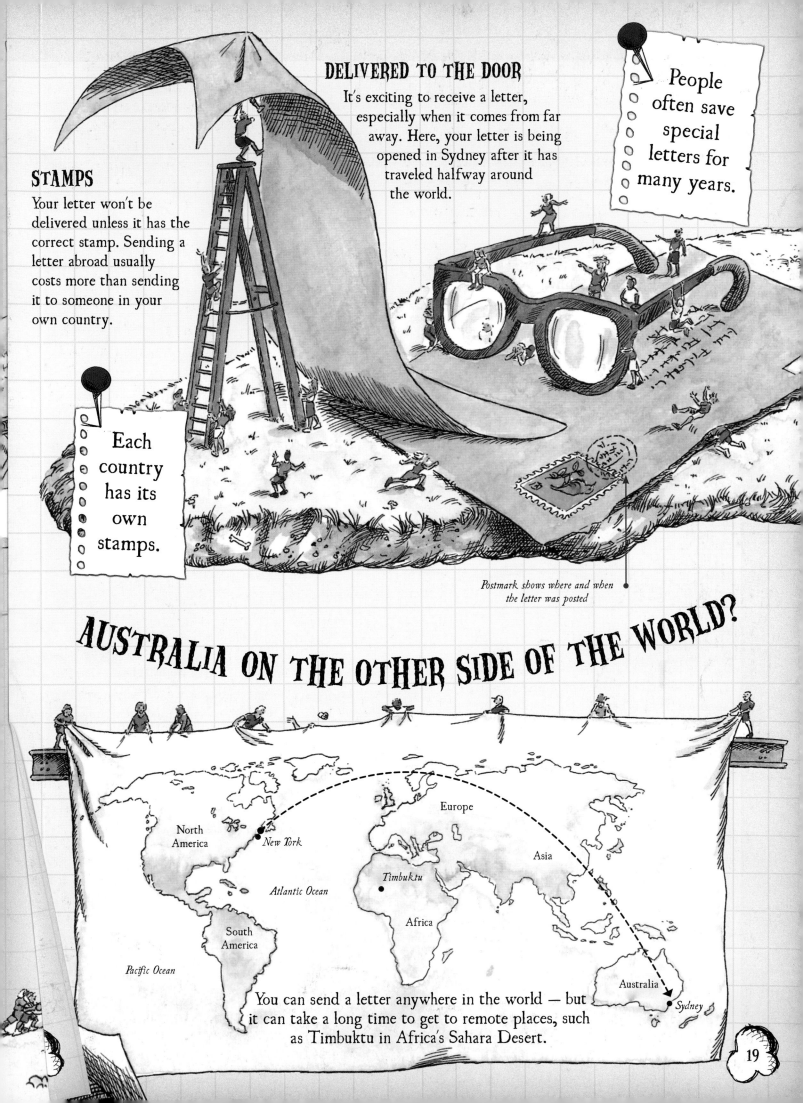

STAMPS

Your letter won't be delivered unless it has the correct stamp. Sending a letter abroad usually costs more than sending it to someone in your own country.

DELIVERED TO THE DOOR

It's exciting to receive a letter, especially when it comes from far away. Here, your letter is being opened in Sydney after it has traveled halfway around the world.

People often save special letters for many years.

Each country has its own stamps.

Postmark shows where and when the letter was posted

AUSTRALIA ON THE OTHER SIDE OF THE WORLD?

North America

New York

Europe

Asia

Atlantic Ocean

Timbuktu

Africa

South America

Pacific Ocean

Australia

Sydney

You can send a letter anywhere in the world — but it can take a long time to get to remote places, such as Timbuktu in Africa's Sahara Desert.

MICROWAVE OVEN

A microwave oven heats food in a fraction of the time it takes a conventional oven, and the oven itself doesn't get hot. Using a device called a magnetron, it fires a powerful form of energy known as **microwaves**.

WHAT ARE MICROWAVES?

Microwaves travel at 186,000 miles per second and can pass through air, food, or empty space. Microwaves from space hit us all the time, but they are so weak that they have no effect on us. The energy used in microwave ovens is much more powerful.

Inner lining

COOKING WITH WAVES

When microwave energy passes through the water **molecules** in food, the molecules begin to move rapidly. This movement produces heat, which cooks the food.

1 COLD

In cold food, water molecules are spread out randomly. They move around, but only slowly.

2 WARM

As microwaves travel through the food, the water molecules move rapidly in different directions.

3 HOT

The rapidly moving molecules produce heat, which spreads through the food and cooks it.

4 INSIDE OUT

The microwaves enter the food and cause it to heat up, so it cooks from the inside out. A conventional oven, by contrast, heats the air around the food.

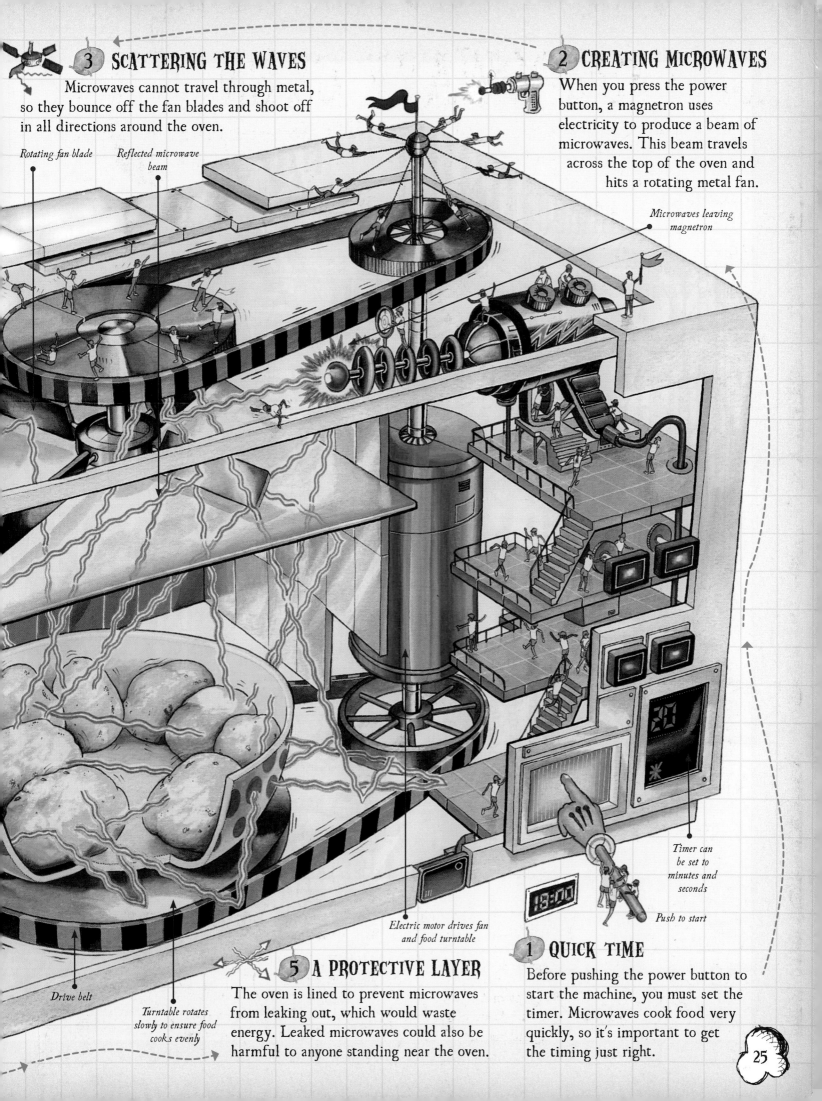

3 SCATTERING THE WAVES

Microwaves cannot travel through metal, so they bounce off the fan blades and shoot off in all directions around the oven.

Rotating fan blade

Reflected microwave beam

2 CREATING MICROWAVES

When you press the power button, a magnetron uses electricity to produce a beam of microwaves. This beam travels across the top of the oven and hits a rotating metal fan.

Microwaves leaving magnetron

Electric motor drives fan and food turntable

Timer can be set to minutes and seconds

Push to start

5 A PROTECTIVE LAYER

The oven is lined to prevent microwaves from leaking out, which would waste energy. Leaked microwaves could also be harmful to anyone standing near the oven.

Drive belt

Turntable rotates slowly to ensure food cooks evenly

1 QUICK TIME

Before pushing the power button to start the machine, you must set the timer. Microwaves cook food very quickly, so it's important to get the timing just right.

25

REFRIGERATOR

A refrigerator is a very important machine because keeping food cold stops it from spoiling. Normally you never see the back of a fridge, but this one has been turned around so you can see all of its working parts.

A fridge works by taking heat from the inside compartment and carrying it to the outside. It does this by continuously pumping a special fluid, called a refrigerant, through a long loop of piping. On its journey, the refrigerant changes from a liquid into a **vapor** and back to a liquid. As it becomes a vapor, the fridge absorbs heat from the food. When it turns back into a liquid, it releases the heat into the kitchen.

1 KEEPING COOL

If you go for a swim and then come out without drying off, you'll soon start to feel cold. This is because the water on your skin, warmed by your body, starts to **evaporate** (turn to vapor) and takes heat away from you. In the same way, a fridge becomes cold as the heat from inside it turns liquid refrigerant into vapor.

2 INTO THE INTERIOR

When the refrigerant enters the freezer, it moves through a narrow **nozzle** into a series of pipes. Inside these pipes, the liquid refrigerant absorbs any heat from inside the freezer, and expands into a vapor. The freezer cools down, and its contents become very cold.

3 BACK TO THE COMPRESSOR

The refrigerant then flows out of the freezer, carrying heat absorbed from the food. Next it travels down to the **compressor** (a small pump), which applies **pressure** to the vaporized refrigerant. The refrigerant is squeezed back into liquid form, and begins to release heat.

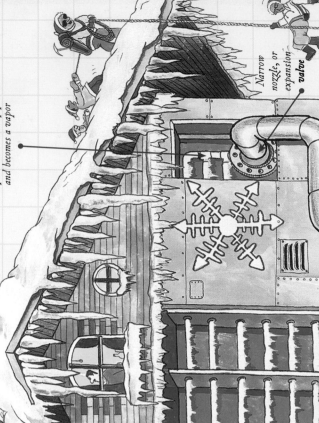

Liquid refrigerant expands into these pipes and becomes a vapor

Narrow nozzle, or expansion valve

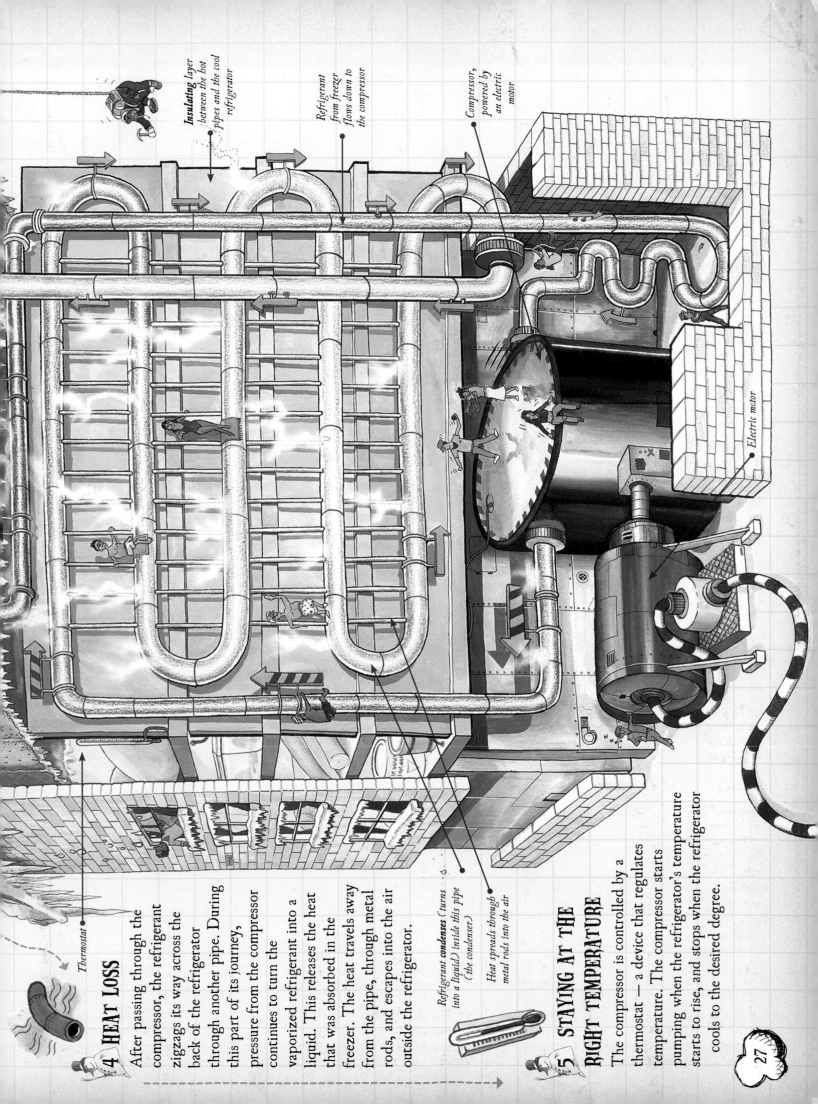

Insulating layer between the hot pipes and the cool refrigerator

Refrigerant from freezer flows down to the compressor

Compressor, powered by an electric motor

Electric motor

Refrigerant **condenses** (turns into a liquid) inside this pipe (the condenser)

Heat spreads through metal rods into the air

Thermostat

4 HEAT LOSS

After passing through the compressor, the refrigerant zigzags its way across the back of the refrigerator through another pipe. During this part of its journey, pressure from the compressor continues to turn the vaporized refrigerant into a liquid. This releases the heat that was absorbed in the freezer. The heat travels away from the pipe, through metal rods, and escapes into the air outside the refrigerator.

5 STAYING AT THE RIGHT TEMPERATURE

The compressor is controlled by a thermostat — a device that regulates temperature. The compressor starts pumping when the refrigerator's temperature starts to rise, and stops when the refrigerator cools to the desired degree.

27

WASHING MACHINE

People used to wash clothes by hand, using rocks from rivers to scrub out the dirt. Technology has made this chore much easier, but what happens to the clothes is still pretty similar. Using drums, springs, belts, **bearings,** and, of course, detergent, the modern washing machine removes the dirt from your clothes and then spins them until they are almost dry. The machine follows special programs that take the clothes through cycles of soaking, washing, and rinsing, until finally they are ready to be put in a tumble dryer or hung on a clothesline to dry.

1 CHOOSING YOUR WASH

The control panel lets you select the right wash program for your clothes. Some fabrics are much more delicate than others, and need a gentler wash. Each program sets the length of the wash cycle, the speed at which the inner drum spins, and the temperature of the water.

2 CHEMICAL CLEANERS

Before you start the machine, you need to put some detergent into it. Detergents contain more than a dozen ingredients. Some help the water soak into clothes, while others remove stains and dirt. Many detergents also contain **enzymes** — chemicals that help break down substances, such as fat or blood, on your clothes.

3 GET IT GOING

The washing machine is driven by an electric motor. (You can find out more about electric motors on page 47).

4 THE DRUM KIT

The motor is connected by a drive belt to the inner drum. When you switch on the machine, the drive belt turns the inner drum, which rotates on ball bearings. The drum is full of holes that allow water to flow into and out of it. As the drum rotates, the clothes move against each other, as well as against the sides of the drum, and it is this agitation, with help from the detergent, that removes the dirt from the clothing. The outer drum cannot move, and forms a watertight compartment when the door is closed.

Detergent drawer

Rubber seal

Safety lock prevents door from opening while machine is switched on

Box of detergent

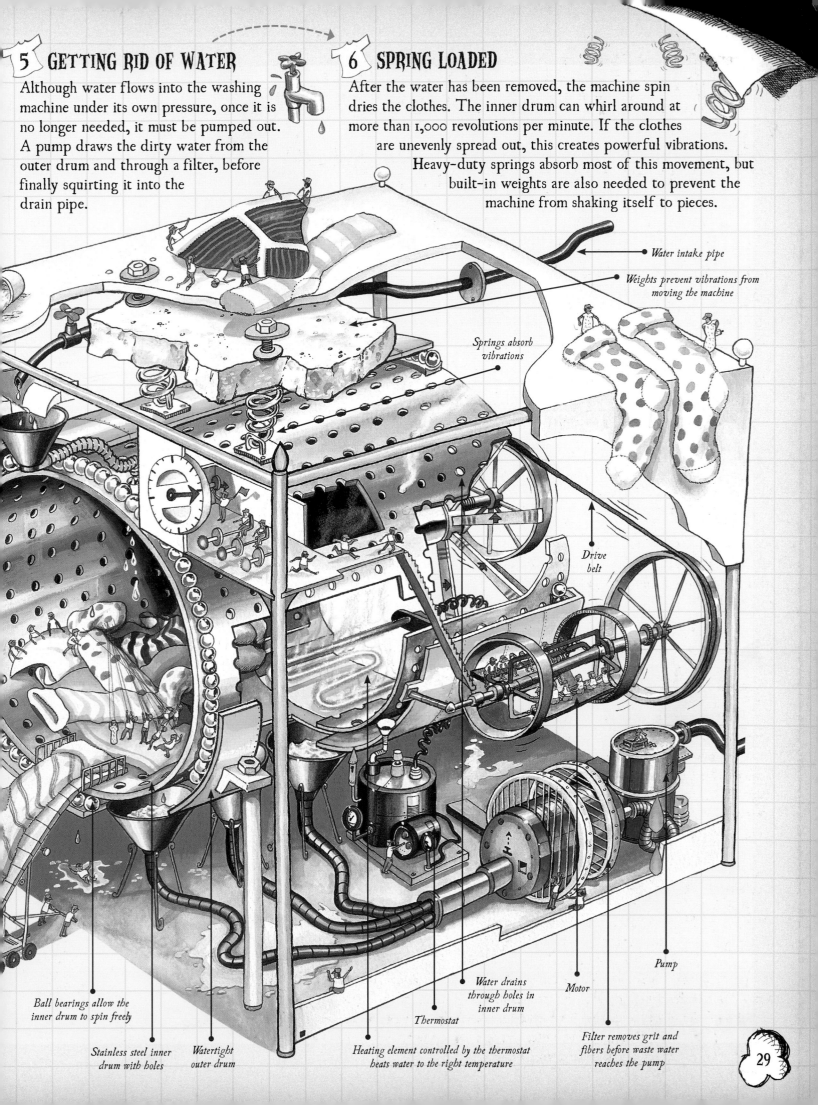

5 GETTING RID OF WATER

Although water flows into the washing machine under its own pressure, once it is no longer needed, it must be pumped out. A pump draws the dirty water from the outer drum and through a filter, before finally squirting it into the drain pipe.

6 SPRING LOADED

After the water has been removed, the machine spin dries the clothes. The inner drum can whirl around at more than 1,000 revolutions per minute. If the clothes are unevenly spread out, this creates powerful vibrations. Heavy-duty springs absorb most of this movement, but built-in weights are also needed to prevent the machine from shaking itself to pieces.

Water intake pipe

Weights prevent vibrations from moving the machine

Springs absorb vibrations

Drive belt

Ball bearings allow the inner drum to spin freely

Stainless steel inner drum with holes

Watertight outer drum

Thermostat

Heating element controlled by the thermostat heats water to the right temperature

Water drains through holes in inner drum

Motor

Pump

Filter removes grit and fibers before waste water reaches the pump

TOASTER

For breakfast lovers, this could be one of the most important machines ever invented. It toasts bread to perfection and automatically turns off when the slices are ready to eat. This cutaway will help answer one of the most pressing questions facing any toast enthusiast. How does the toaster know when the toast is done? The answer lies in a tiny device called a bimetallic strip, which responds to heat by changing shape. The strip is set to release a catch at just the right moment, popping up the toast and preventing it from burning.

5 TIMED TO PERFECTION

Some toasters are controlled by a timer instead of a bimetallic strip. When the timer reaches zero, it activates a switch that turns on the electromagnet. (To find out more about electromagnets see page 58).

4 TRIPPING THE CATCH

When electricity flows through the toaster's wire coils, it produces a powerful magnetic field. The field attracts a metal catch, and when this catch moves, it releases the lever that holds the toast down.

6 READY FOR LIFTOFF

When you put bread in the toaster and push down the handle, you stretch a pair of metal springs. This causes a catch near the handle to engage with a hinged metal bar, and the bread is held in position. When the toast is ready, the metal bar is released, the spring contracts, and the toast shoots skyward.

1 TURNING ON THE HEAT

Bread is toasted by electric elements that are backed by a heat-resistant shield. The shield keeps the case from getting hot by reflecting heat back toward the toast.

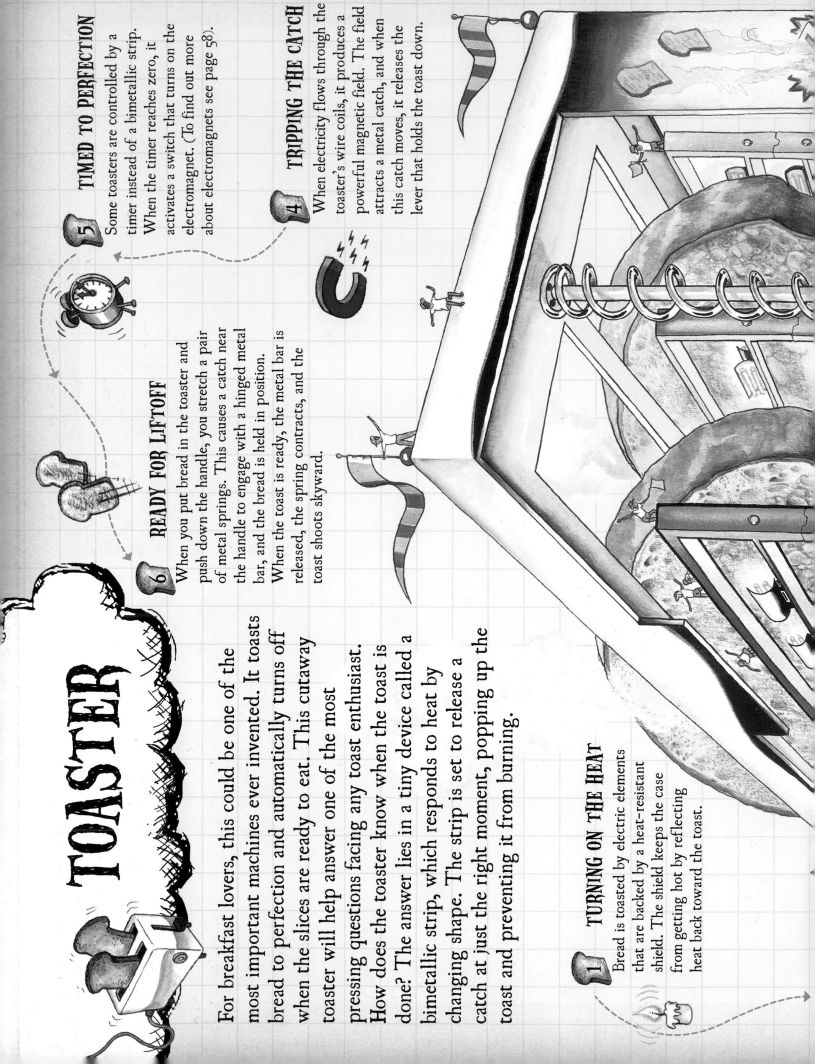

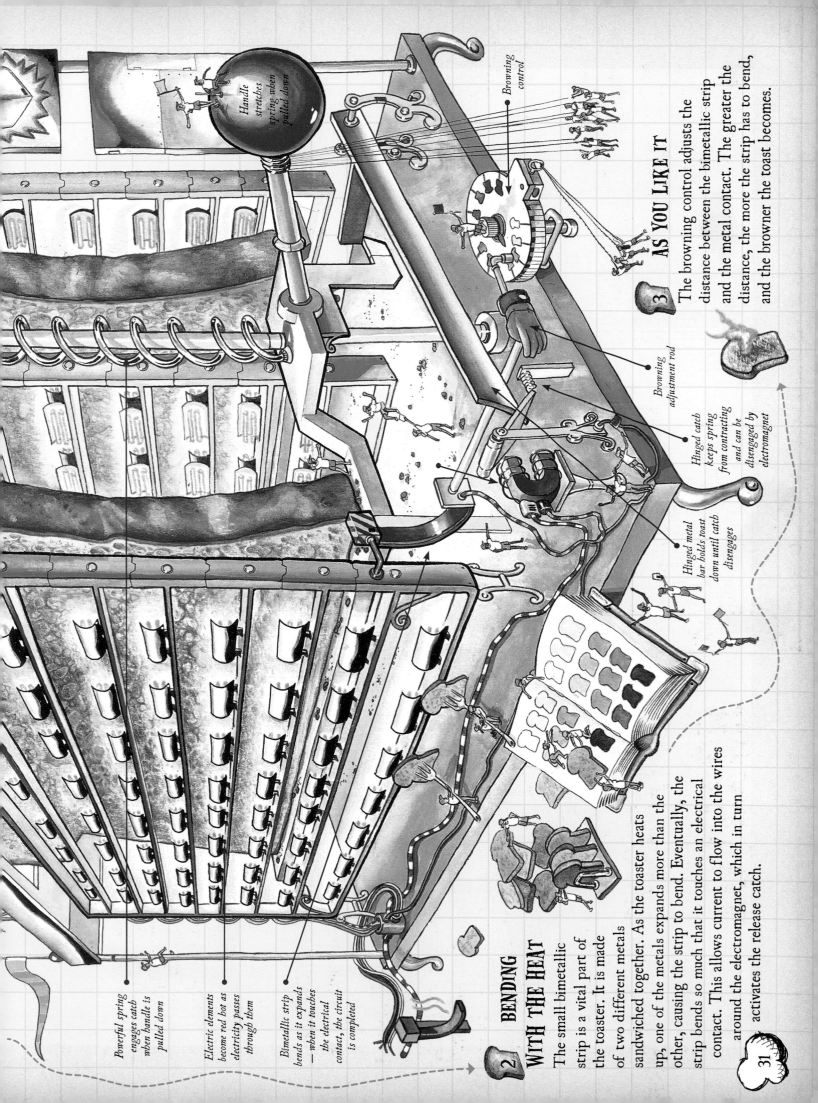

Handle stretches spring when pulled down

Browning control

3 AS YOU LIKE IT

The browning control adjusts the distance between the bimetallic strip and the metal contact. The greater the distance, the more the strip has to bend, and the browner the toast becomes.

Browning adjustment rod

Hinged catch keeps spring from contracting and can be disengaged by electromagnet

Hinged metal bar holds toast down until catch disengages

Powerful spring engages catch when handle is pulled down

Electric elements become red hot as electricity passes through them

Bimetallic strip bends as it expands — when it touches the electrical contact, the circuit is completed

2 BENDING WITH THE HEAT

The small bimetallic strip is a vital part of the toaster. It is made of two different metals sandwiched together. As the toaster heats up, one of the metals expands more than the other, causing the strip to bend. Eventually, the strip bends so much that it touches an electrical contact. This allows current to flow into the wires around the electromagnet, which in turn activates the release catch.

31

FOOD PROCESSOR

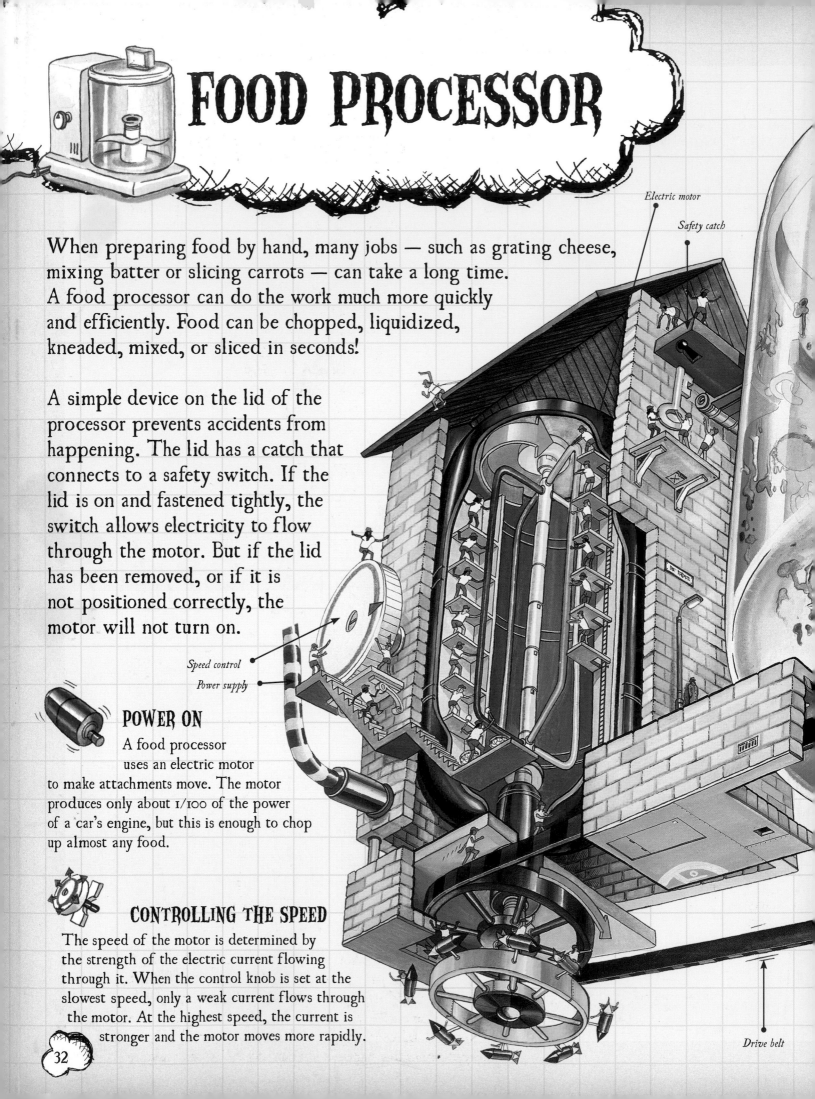

When preparing food by hand, many jobs — such as grating cheese, mixing batter or slicing carrots — can take a long time. A food processor can do the work much more quickly and efficiently. Food can be chopped, liquidized, kneaded, mixed, or sliced in seconds!

A simple device on the lid of the processor prevents accidents from happening. The lid has a catch that connects to a safety switch. If the lid is on and fastened tightly, the switch allows electricity to flow through the motor. But if the lid has been removed, or if it is not positioned correctly, the motor will not turn on.

Electric motor

Safety catch

Speed control

Power supply

POWER ON

A food processor uses an electric motor to make attachments move. The motor produces only about 1/100 of the power of a car's engine, but this is enough to chop up almost any food.

CONTROLLING THE SPEED

The speed of the motor is determined by the strength of the electric current flowing through it. When the control knob is set at the slowest speed, only a weak current flows through the motor. At the highest speed, the current is stronger and the motor moves more rapidly.

Drive belt

INGREDIENTS FOR THE PIZZA BASE

WHEAT

Wheat is grown from seed, and cut when it is ripe.

Threshing

Winnowing shakes the grains out of their husks.

The grain is milled (ground) to make a fine powder — in the past, heavy stones were used. The powder is the flour used to make the pizza base.

SALT

Salt is found under the ground. Huge blocks of it are cut at salt mines.

The blocks of salt are ground up, and the tiny salt crystals are then dried, and packed.

At the pizzeria, the salt is poured into salt shakers, ready for use.

YEAST

Yeast is a fungus. It is grown in warm tubs, or vats.

When it's ready, the yeast is removed from the vats, dried and cut into chunks, called cakes.

The dried yeast cakes are then wrapped, ready for sale.

OLIVE OIL

Olives grow on trees in some warm countries.

They are picked from the trees and then squeezed in a screw press.

All of the juice runs out of the olives and is collected in bottles. The juice is called olive oil.

The olive oil is delivered to the pizzeria.

SUGAR

Sugar comes from a plant called sugarcane. When the cane is ripe, it is cut.

The sugarcane is crushed to extract the juice. This is boiled until the water in the juice has evaporated, leaving behind sugar crystals.

Blocks of sugar crystals are cut into cubes.

PIZZA TIME

You might find it annoying to have to wait an hour to get your pizza, but it actually takes about a year to grow and collect all of the ingredients.

1 MADE TO ORDER

As soon as you call the pizzeria with your order, the pizza chefs jump into action. First, they mix yeast, sugar, water, and a little flour. Then they let the mixture settle.

Getting the ingredients from the store

Yeast

Flour

Water

3 BUBBLE POWER

Next, the mixture is poured into a bowl with olive oil, some salt, and more flour to make a dough. The bubbles are like millions of tiny balloons. They make the dough light and airy. Without the gas bubbles, the pizza dough would be thick and heavy.

2 GETTING FROTHY

Yeast makes the sugar **ferment**. This means that the sugar turns into alcohol and releases gas bubbles called carbon dioxide, which make the mixture frothy.

The yeast mixture ferments

Yeast mixture

Olive oil

Salt

Flour

4 KNEADING TIME

The dough is placed on a board, and the chef kneads it, pushing and squeezing it into a smooth lump.

Dough

Mixing the ingredients for the dough

Kneading the dough

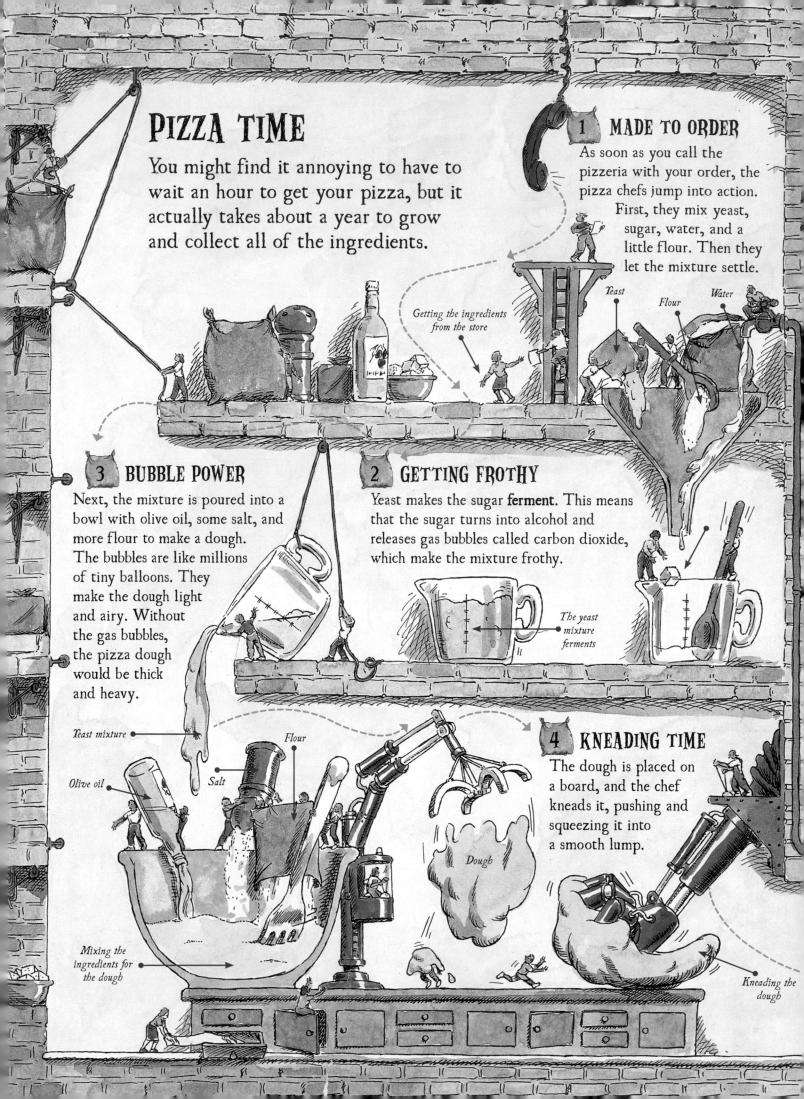

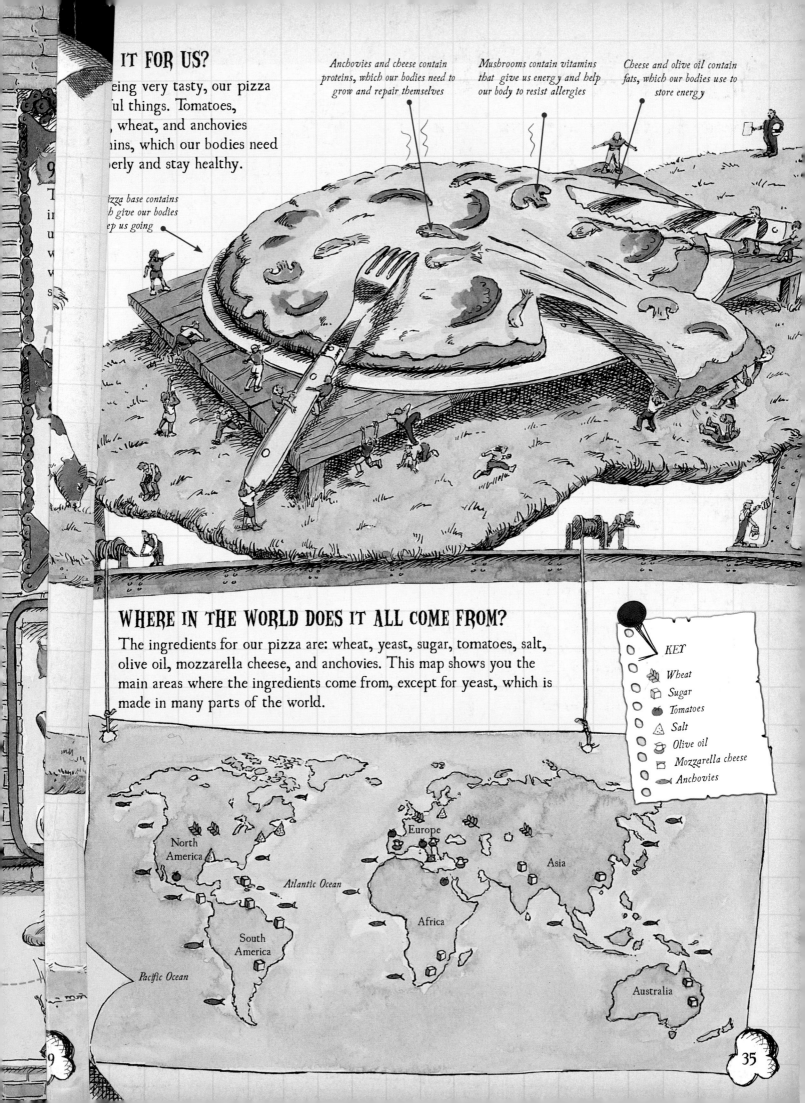

IT FOR US?

...eing very tasty, our pizza
...ul things. Tomatoes,
..., wheat, and anchovies
...ins, which our bodies need
...erly and stay healthy.

...izza base contains
...h give our bodies
...ep us going

Anchovies and cheese contain proteins, which our bodies need to grow and repair themselves

Mushrooms contain vitamins that give us energy and help our body to resist allergies

Cheese and olive oil contain fats, which our bodies use to store energy

WHERE IN THE WORLD DOES IT ALL COME FROM?

The ingredients for our pizza are: wheat, yeast, sugar, tomatoes, salt, olive oil, mozzarella cheese, and anchovies. This map shows you the main areas where the ingredients come from, except for yeast, which is made in many parts of the world.

KEY

Wheat
Sugar
Tomatoes
Salt
Olive oil
Mozzarella cheese
Anchovies

North America

Europe

Asia

Atlantic Ocean

Africa

South America

Pacific Ocean

Australia

VACUUM CLEANER

Twenty-four hours a day, an invisible blizzard piles up dust inside our homes. Some of the dust blows in when we open doors or windows, but a lot of it comes from tiny fibers that break away from our clothes and microscopic flakes that wear away from the surface of our skin. If dust is not cleaned away, it quickly builds up on surfaces all over the house. Fortunately, there is an easy way to get rid of it. The vacuum cleaner creates **suction** that collects these particles of dust, packing them into a bag that can then be thrown away.

6 A BAGFUL OF DUST

The bag is made of a special material that allows air to flow through while keeping dust and dirt inside. As the bag fills with dust and dirt, it becomes more difficult for air to flow through. As a result, there is less suction and the vacuum does not clean as well.

5 FULL OF DIRT?

Each time the vacuum cleaner is turned on, the dust bag swells up like a balloon. This is because the pressure of the air inside the bag becomes greater than the **air pressure** around it.

On/off switch

Airtight compartment

Pipe

A second filter ensures that all the dust and dirt is removed before the air leaves the machine

4 CLEANING BY SUCTION

The dust bag is in a compartment in the upper part of the vacuum cleaner, along with a filter. The compartment is airtight, but the dust bag contains tiny holes that let air flow through to a fan underneath. When the machine is switched on, the fan sucks air out of the compartment, producing a partial vacuum. The resulting suction pulls air and dirt through the pipe and into the bag.

Disposable bag traps dirt and dust while allowing air to pass through

Fan sucks air out of airtight compartment

3 DUST ON THE MOVE

Once the dust has been dislodged from the carpet, it is sucked into a pipe. The pipe carries it through the machine and into the dust bag.

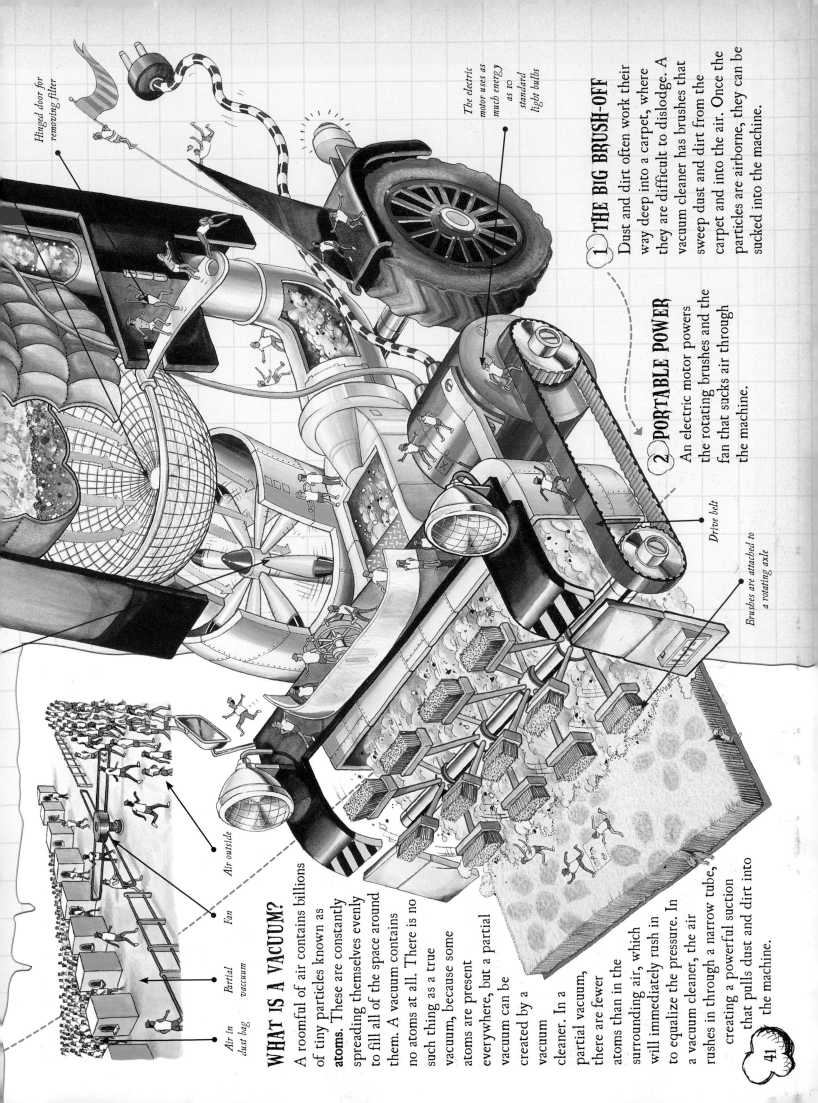

The electric
motor uses as
much energy
as 10
standard
light bulbs

1 THE BIG BRUSH-OFF

Dust and dirt often work their
way deep into a carpet, where
they are difficult to dislodge. A
vacuum cleaner has brushes that
sweep dust and dirt from the
carpet and into the air. Once the
particles are airborne, they can be
sucked into the machine.

2 PORTABLE POWER

An electric motor powers
the rotating brushes and the
fan that sucks air through
the machine.

Drive belt

Brushes are attached to
a rotating axle

Air outside

Fan

Partial
vacuum

Air in
dust bag

WHAT IS A VACUUM?

A roomful of air contains billions
of tiny particles known as
atoms. These are constantly
spreading themselves evenly
to fill all of the space around
them. A vacuum contains
no atoms at all. There is no
such thing as a true
vacuum, because some
atoms are present
everywhere, but a partial
vacuum can be
created by a
vacuum
cleaner. In a
partial vacuum,
there are fewer
atoms than in the
surrounding air, which
will immediately rush in
to equalize the pressure. In
a vacuum cleaner, the air
rushes in through a narrow tube,
creating a powerful suction
that pulls dust and dirt into
the machine.

41

SEWING MACHINE

The inside of a sewing machine is like a frantic factory where many things are happening at once. Axles spin, belts hum, rods clatter, and the needle moves up and down with blinding speed. But behind this seeming chaos is a series of carefully designed movements, all powered by a single electric motor. In less time than it takes you to blink, a sewing machine makes a stitch, tightens it and moves the fabric forward in preparation for the next stitch.

MAKING THINGS MOVE

Sewing machines today are powered by small electric motors. (To find out more about electric motors, see page 47.) The motor turns an axle, which is linked to the rest of the moving parts within the sewing machine. Devices called cranks and **cams** convert the rotational movement of the axle into the up-and-down movement of the needle.

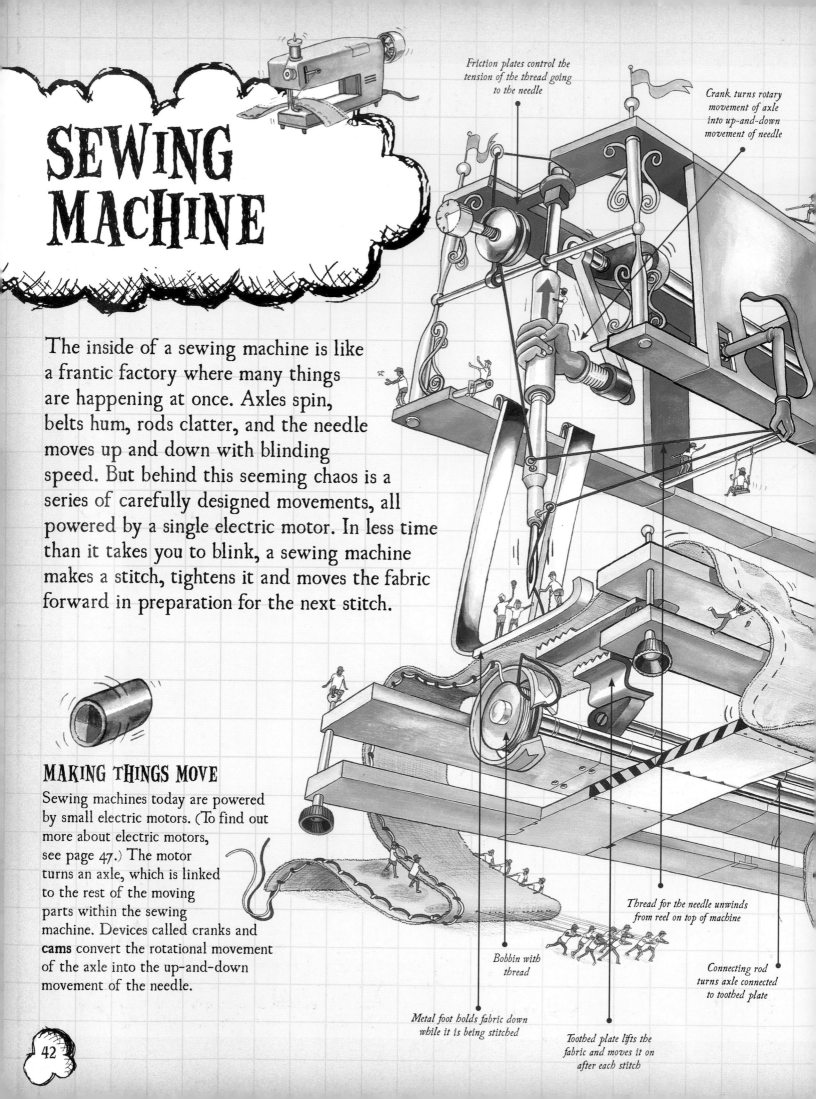

Friction plates control the tension of the thread going to the needle

Crank turns rotary movement of axle into up-and-down movement of needle

Thread for the needle unwinds from reel on top of machine

Connecting rod turns axle connected to toothed plate

Bobbin with thread

Metal foot holds fabric down while it is being stitched

Toothed plate lifts the fabric and moves it on after each stitch

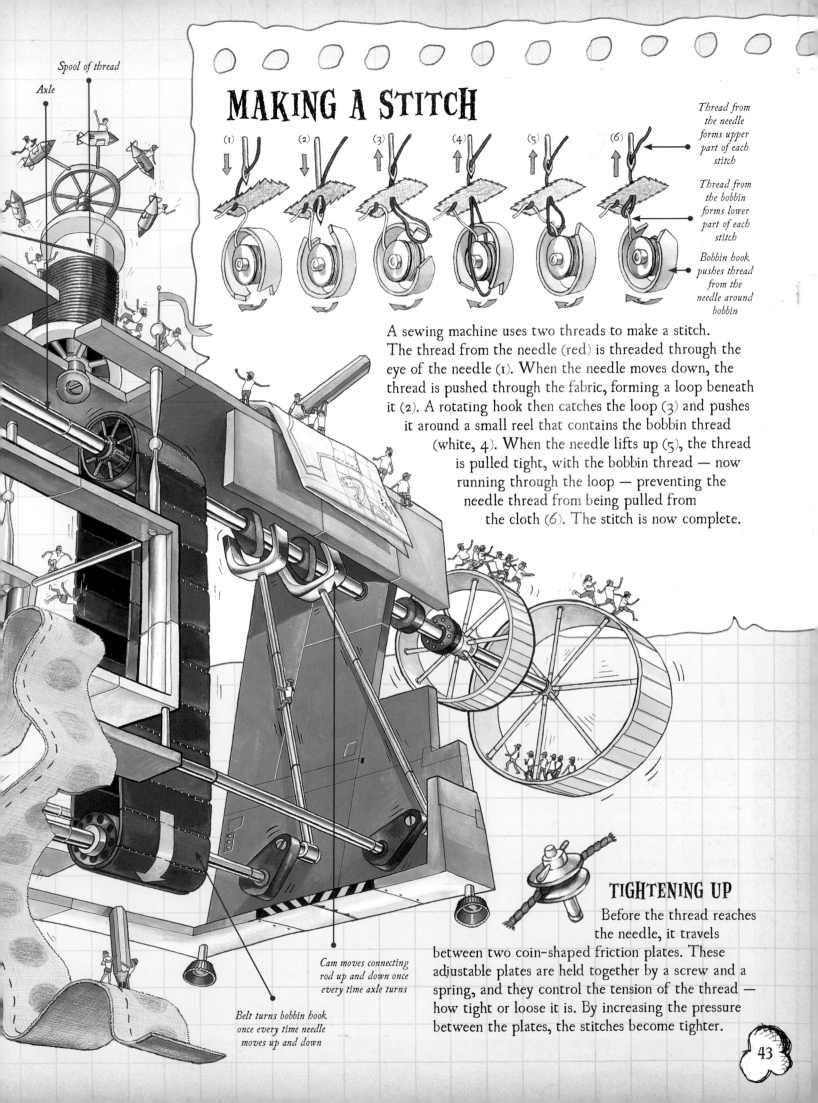

Spool of thread

Axle

MAKING A STITCH

(1) (2) (3) (4) (5) (6)

Thread from the needle forms upper part of each stitch

Thread from the bobbin forms lower part of each stitch

Bobbin hook pushes thread from the needle around bobbin

A sewing machine uses two threads to make a stitch. The thread from the needle (red) is threaded through the eye of the needle (1). When the needle moves down, the thread is pushed through the fabric, forming a loop beneath it (2). A rotating hook then catches the loop (3) and pushes it around a small reel that contains the bobbin thread (white, 4). When the needle lifts up (5), the thread is pulled tight, with the bobbin thread — now running through the loop — preventing the needle thread from being pulled from the cloth (6). The stitch is now complete.

Cam moves connecting rod up and down once every time axle turns

Belt turns bobbin hook once every time needle moves up and down

TIGHTENING UP

Before the thread reaches the needle, it travels between two coin-shaped friction plates. These adjustable plates are held together by a screw and a spring, and they control the tension of the thread — how tight or loose it is. By increasing the pressure between the plates, the stitches become tighter.

TOILET TANK

Air-filled float attached to valve control arm

The toilet tank is something that we see every day, but rarely look into. Inside, the tank has two simple but effective devices that make the toilet work: a float and a siphon. The float, seen on the left of this tank, ensures that the water fills to the proper level, and no higher. The siphon, in the center, draws water into the toilet bowl in a continuous flow. Now, are you ready to take the plunge and find out what happens when you flush the toilet?

HOW A SIPHON WORKS

A siphon is a tube in which a liquid is drawn up a short distance before flowing down to a lower level. In a toilet, it's the siphon tube that carries water from the tank to the toilet bowl below. A siphon works because of suction — this is when air is removed from a space and a liquid takes its place. Water will flow continuoulsy through a siphon so long as the tube remains full of water, and the water is flowing from a higher level to a lower level. As soon as air enters the siphon, the suction is broken and the flow of water stops.

1 MAKING WATER MOVE

The toilet handle is connected to a piston (two sliding discs) inside the siphon bell. When you push on the toilet handle, a lever pulls these discs up, forcing water into the siphon tube. This provides suction, which draws the rest of the water in the tank up into the tube as well. From there, the water quickly flows down into the toilet bowl. As the tank empties, the float falls to the bottom of the tank.

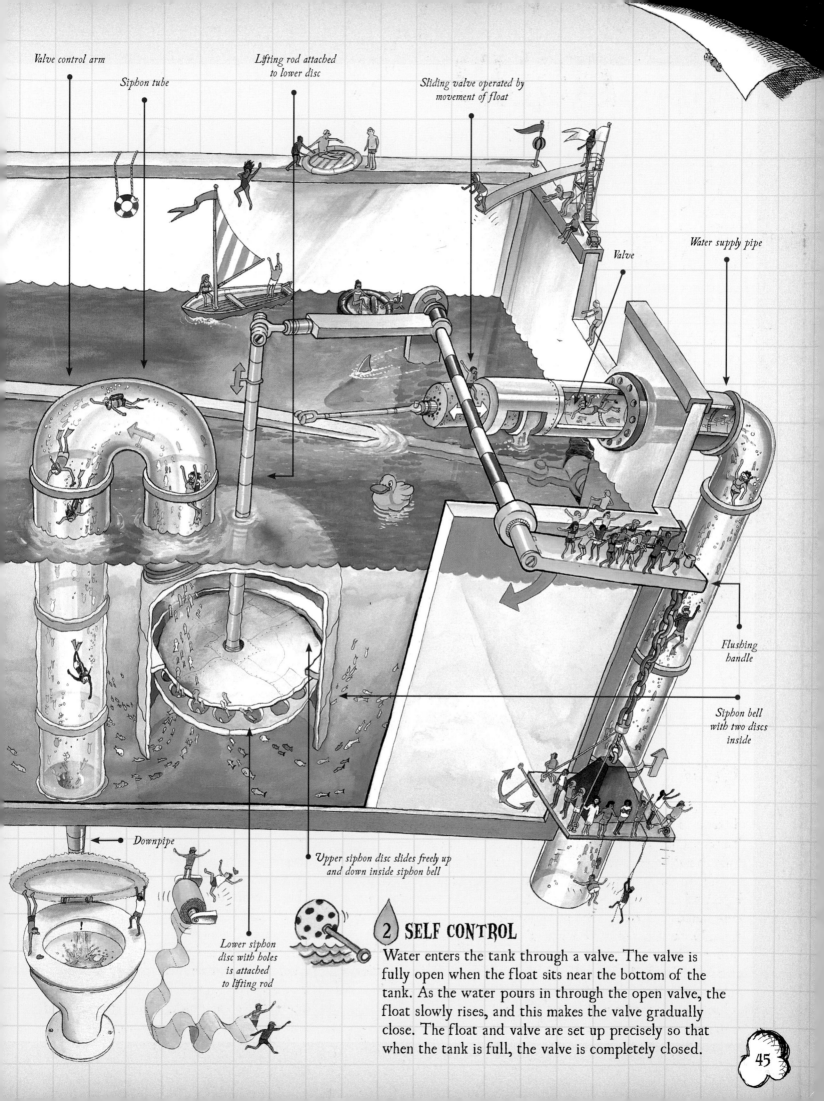

Valve control arm

Siphon tube

Lifting rod attached
to lower disc

Sliding valve operated by
movement of float

Valve

Water supply pipe

Flushing
handle

Siphon bell
with two discs
inside

Downpipe

Upper siphon disc slides freely up
and down inside siphon bell

Lower siphon
disc with holes
is attached
to lifting rod

2 SELF CONTROL

Water enters the tank through a valve. The valve is
fully open when the float sits near the bottom of the
tank. As the water pours in through the open valve, the
float slowly rises, and this makes the valve gradually
close. The float and valve are set up precisely so that
when the tank is full, the valve is completely closed.

45

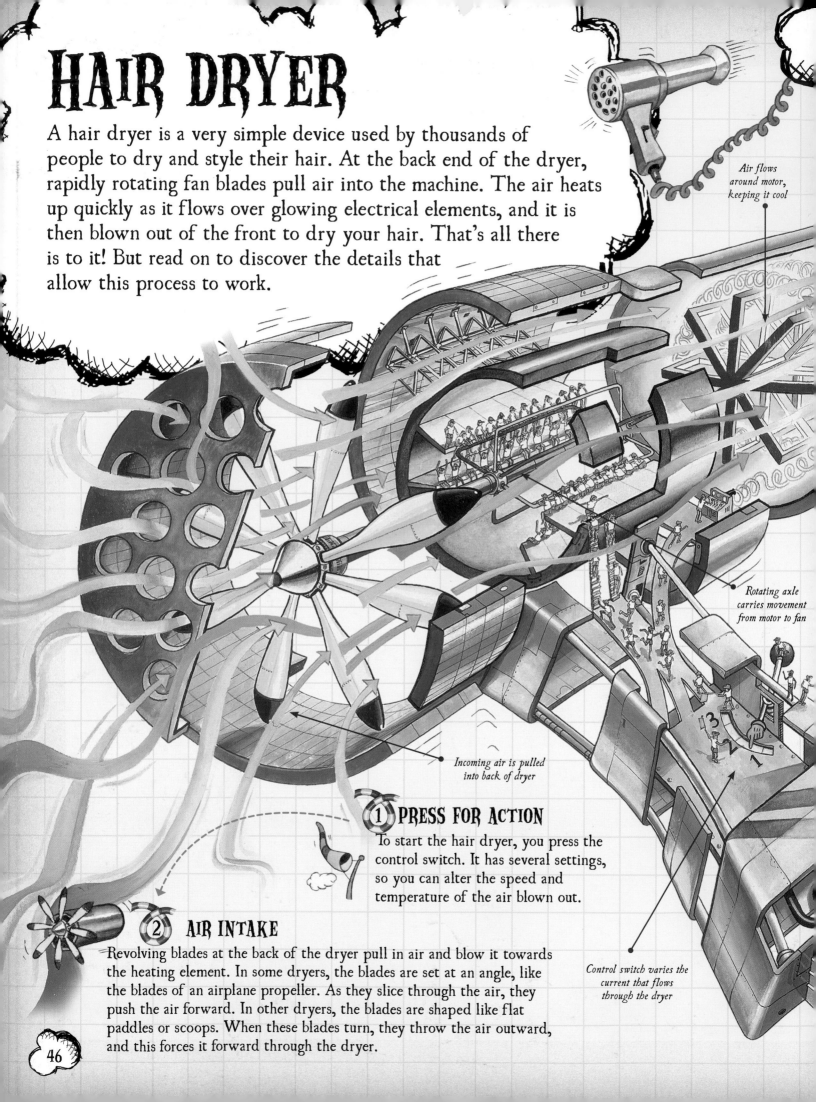

HAIR DRYER

A hair dryer is a very simple device used by thousands of people to dry and style their hair. At the back end of the dryer, rapidly rotating fan blades pull air into the machine. The air heats up quickly as it flows over glowing electrical elements, and it is then blown out of the front to dry your hair. That's all there is to it! But read on to discover the details that allow this process to work.

Air flows around motor, keeping it cool

Rotating axle carries movement from motor to fan

Incoming air is pulled into back of dryer

① PRESS FOR ACTION

To start the hair dryer, you press the control switch. It has several settings, so you can alter the speed and temperature of the air blown out.

② AIR INTAKE

Revolving blades at the back of the dryer pull in air and blow it towards the heating element. In some dryers, the blades are set at an angle, like the blades of an airplane propeller. As they slice through the air, they push the air forward. In other dryers, the blades are shaped like flat paddles or scoops. When these blades turn, they throw the air outward, and this forces it forward through the dryer.

Control switch varies the current that flows through the dryer

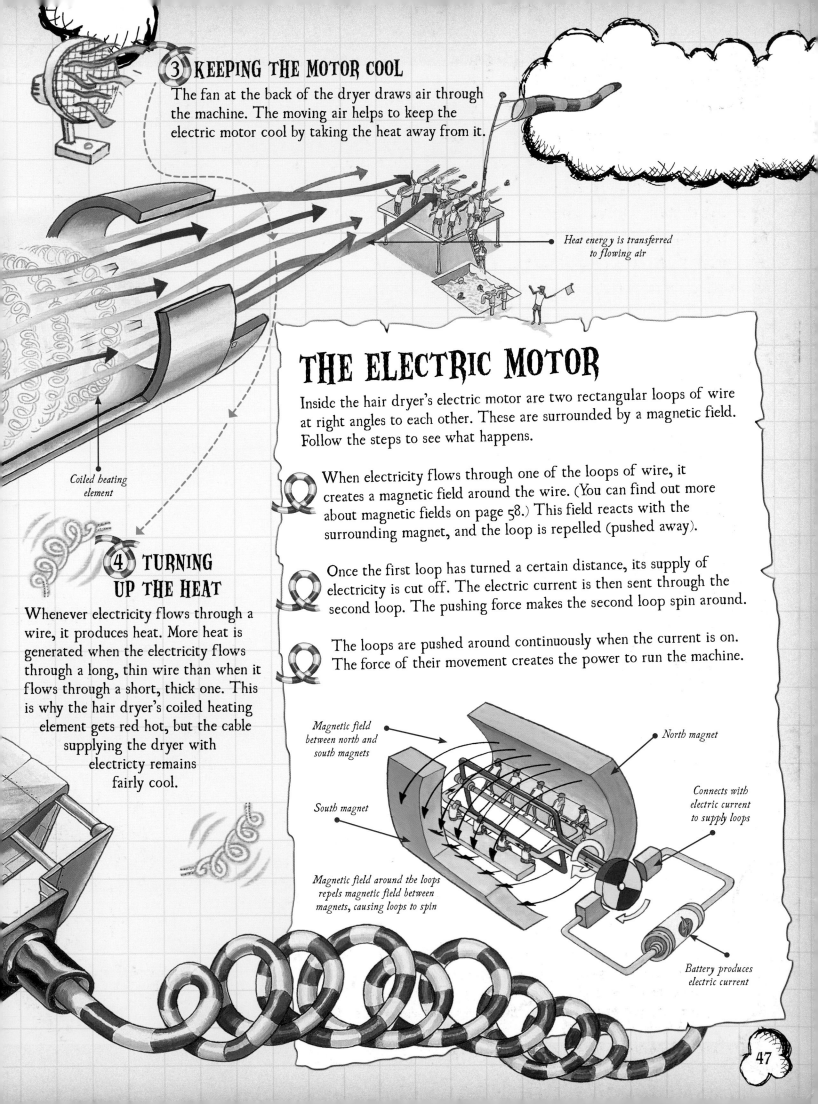

③ KEEPING THE MOTOR COOL

The fan at the back of the dryer draws air through the machine. The moving air helps to keep the electric motor cool by taking the heat away from it.

Heat energy is transferred to flowing air

Coiled heating element

④ TURNING UP THE HEAT

Whenever electricity flows through a wire, it produces heat. More heat is generated when the electricity flows through a long, thin wire than when it flows through a short, thick one. This is why the hair dryer's coiled heating element gets red hot, but the cable supplying the dryer with electricty remains fairly cool.

THE ELECTRIC MOTOR

Inside the hair dryer's electric motor are two rectangular loops of wire at right angles to each other. These are surrounded by a magnetic field. Follow the steps to see what happens.

When electricity flows through one of the loops of wire, it creates a magnetic field around the wire. (You can find out more about magnetic fields on page 58.) This field reacts with the surrounding magnet, and the loop is repelled (pushed away).

Once the first loop has turned a certain distance, its supply of electricity is cut off. The electric current is then sent through the second loop. The pushing force makes the second loop spin around.

The loops are pushed around continuously when the current is on. The force of their movement creates the power to run the machine.

Magnetic field between north and south magnets

North magnet

South magnet

Connects with electric current to supply loops

Magnetic field around the loops repels magnetic field between magnets, causing loops to spin

Battery produces electric current

SMOKE ALARM

Just as there is no smoke without fire, there is rarely a fire without smoke. Because smoke spreads very quickly, it is often the first sign that a fire has broken out.

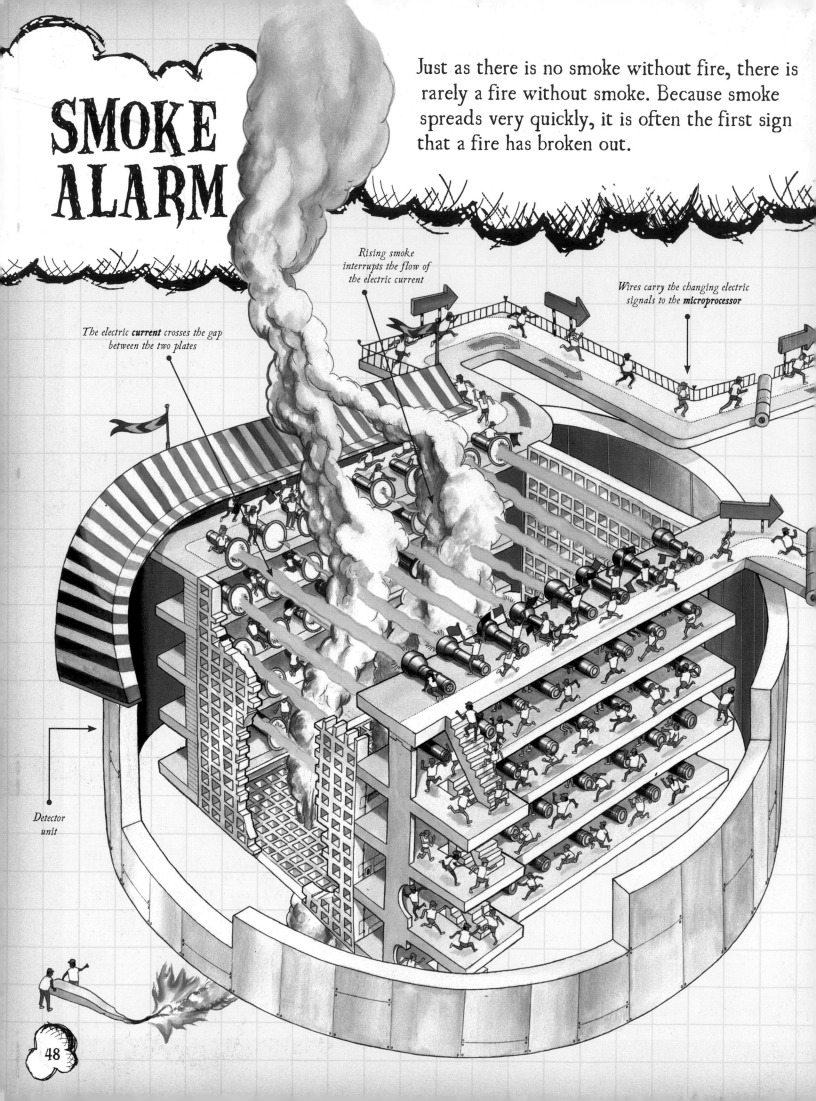

Rising smoke interrupts the flow of the electric current

*Wires carry the changing electric signals to the **microprocessor***

*The electric **current** crosses the gap between the two plates*

Detector unit

The human nose is sensitive and is good at smelling smoke — but only when it is very near. What if a fire were to start on the other side of a shut door, or you were asleep, or you had a cold and couldn't smell the smoke? This is when a smoke detector comes in handy. As soon as it senses smoke, an alarm is triggered that blasts throughout the house.

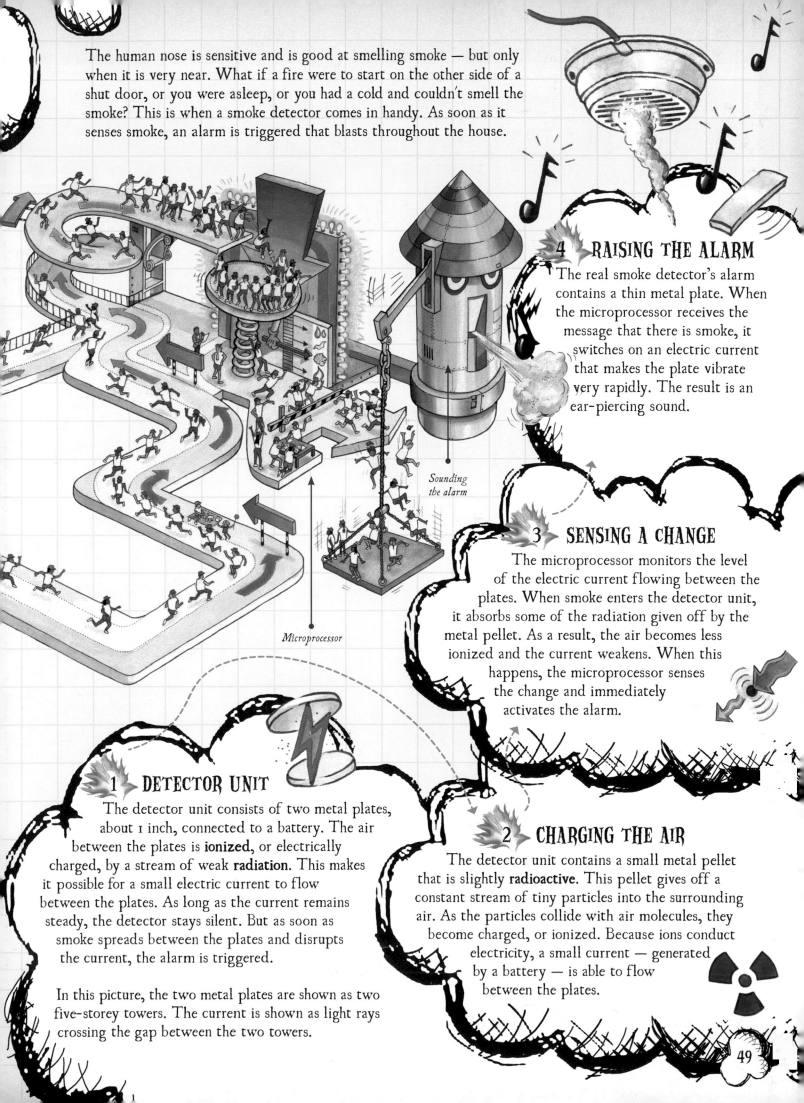

Microprocessor

Sounding the alarm

4 ▸ RAISING THE ALARM

The real smoke detector's alarm contains a thin metal plate. When the microprocessor receives the message that there is smoke, it switches on an electric current that makes the plate vibrate very rapidly. The result is an ear-piercing sound.

3 ▸ SENSING A CHANGE

The microprocessor monitors the level of the electric current flowing between the plates. When smoke enters the detector unit, it absorbs some of the radiation given off by the metal pellet. As a result, the air becomes less ionized and the current weakens. When this happens, the microprocessor senses the change and immediately activates the alarm.

1 ▸ DETECTOR UNIT

The detector unit consists of two metal plates, about 1 inch, connected to a battery. The air between the plates is **ionized,** or electrically charged, by a stream of weak **radiation.** This makes it possible for a small electric current to flow between the plates. As long as the current remains steady, the detector stays silent. But as soon as smoke spreads between the plates and disrupts the current, the alarm is triggered.

In this picture, the two metal plates are shown as two five-storey towers. The current is shown as light rays crossing the gap between the two towers.

2 ▸ CHARGING THE AIR

The detector unit contains a small metal pellet that is slightly **radioactive.** This pellet gives off a constant stream of tiny particles into the surrounding air. As the particles collide with air molecules, they become charged, or ionized. Because ions conduct electricity, a small current — generated by a battery — is able to flow between the plates.

USING A CELL PHONE

By 2015, around 2.7 billion people worldwide owned a smartphone. These amazing cell phones – which connect to the Internet, run little programs called **apps**, play games, take photos, and capture video – are now one of the most important gadgets on the planet. So how do they work and what can you do with them?

1 OPERATING SYSTEM

All smartphones use an **operating system**. This controls all the different parts of the phone — for example the **touchscreen**, the memory where everything is stored and the processor (the "brain" of the phone) — and makes sure they work in harmony with all the apps you use every day. The operating system also controls all the phone's electronics, so it knows to start recharging when you plug it into the outlet, or to turn the speaker off when you plug in your headphones.

2 BATTERY

The first cell phones had batteries that were many times bigger than the phone. Often the phone was clipped to the top of the battery, which had a big carrying handle, like a lunchbox! Modern batteries are tiny, they recharge in a couple of hours and they last all day.

3 USB CONNECTOR

A modern smartphone has a single connector attached to a Universal Serial Bus (USB) cable. When you need to recharge your phone, all you do is plug this connector into a standard outlet. You can also plug the connector directly into your computer, so you can download photos from your phone and keep them safe.

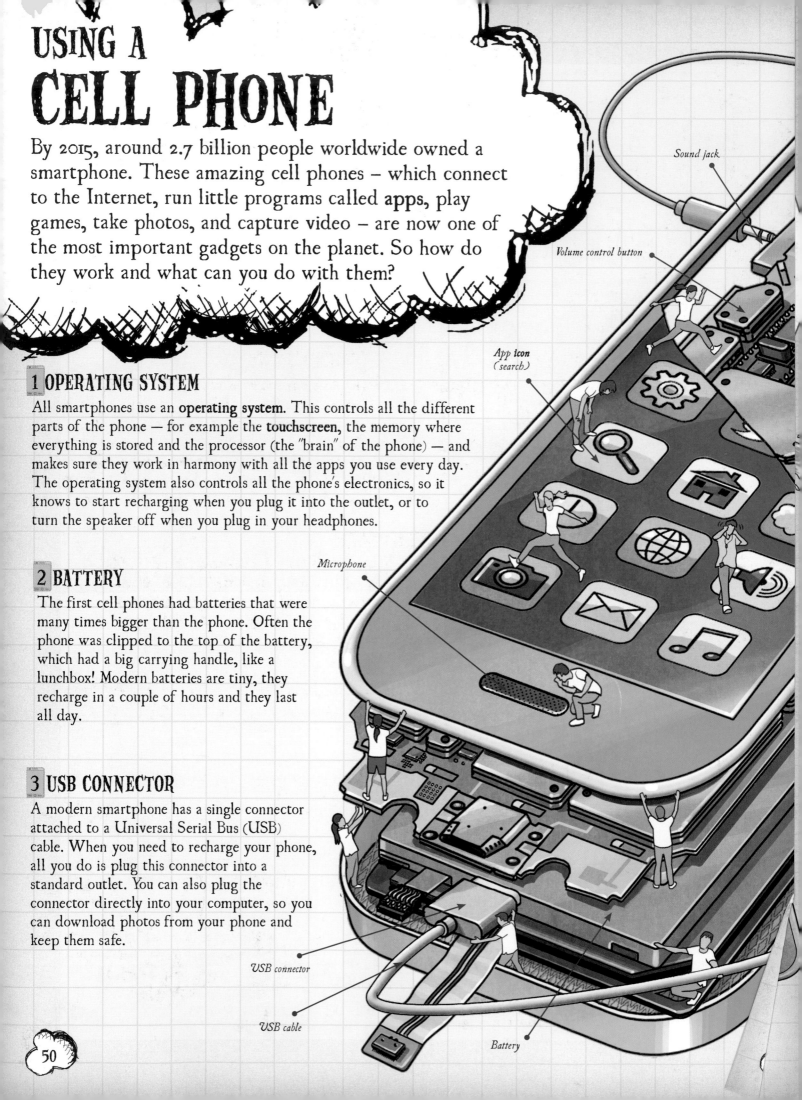

Sound jack

Volume control button

App **icon**
(search)

Microphone

USB connector

USB cable

Battery

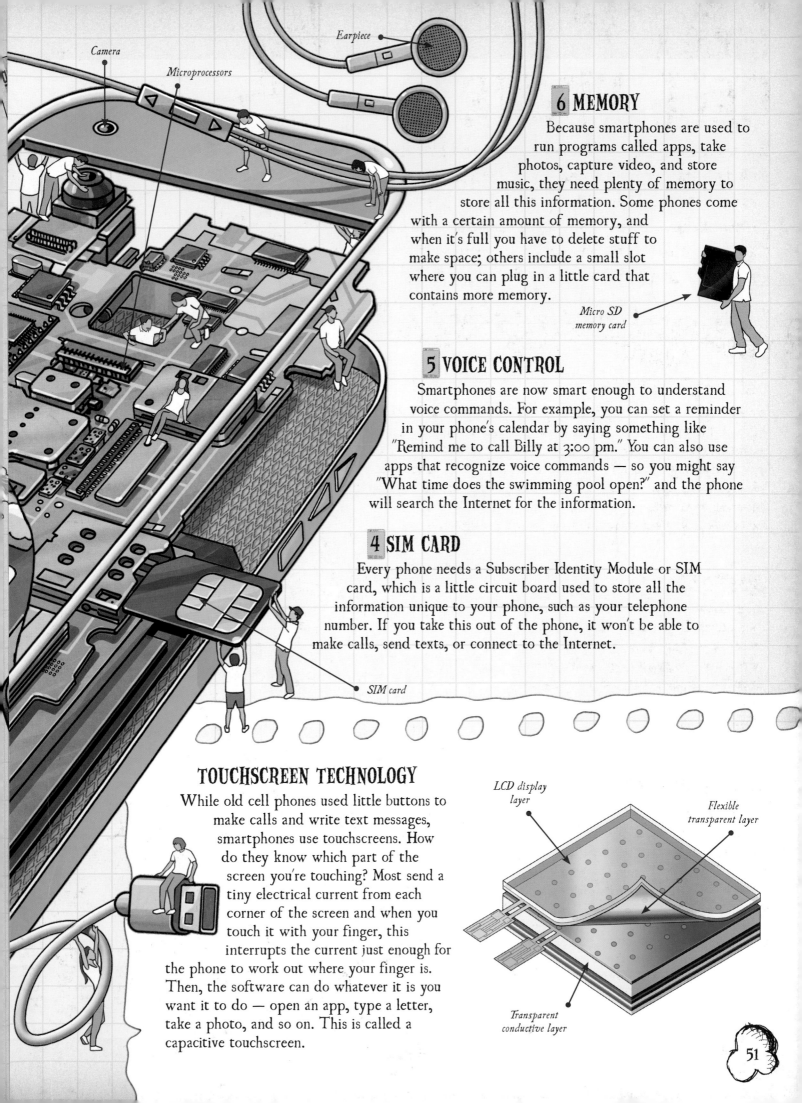

Camera

Microprocessors

Earpiece

6 MEMORY

Because smartphones are used to run programs called apps, take photos, capture video, and store music, they need plenty of memory to store all this information. Some phones come with a certain amount of memory, and when it's full you have to delete stuff to make space; others include a small slot where you can plug in a little card that contains more memory.

Micro SD
memory card

5 VOICE CONTROL

Smartphones are now smart enough to understand voice commands. For example, you can set a reminder in your phone's calendar by saying something like "Remind me to call Billy at 3:00 pm." You can also use apps that recognize voice commands — so you might say "What time does the swimming pool open?" and the phone will search the Internet for the information.

4 SIM CARD

Every phone needs a Subscriber Identity Module or SIM card, which is a little circuit board used to store all the information unique to your phone, such as your telephone number. If you take this out of the phone, it won't be able to make calls, send texts, or connect to the Internet.

SIM card

TOUCHSCREEN TECHNOLOGY

While old cell phones used little buttons to make calls and write text messages, smartphones use touchscreens. How do they know which part of the screen you're touching? Most send a tiny electrical current from each corner of the screen and when you touch it with your finger, this interrupts the current just enough for the phone to work out where your finger is. Then, the software can do whatever it is you want it to do — open an app, type a letter, take a photo, and so on. This is called a capacitive touchscreen.

LCD display
layer

Flexible
transparent layer

Transparent
conductive layer

51

SOLAR PANELS

When it comes to producing energy, the sun is in a league of its own. Just 1 hour of sunlight provides more energy than everyone on planet Earth uses in an entire year. Solar panels are able to convert that energy into something useful, such as a nice hot shower or an hour in front of your favorite TV show. Here's how they work.

1 ENERGY FROM THE SUN

Solar energy can be used either to heat water or to make electricity. When it's used to heat water — for baths, showers, or warming the house — it's called solar thermal energy. When it's used to make electricity to run our gadgets and household appliances, it's called solar voltaic energy.

Solar thermal panel

Solar voltaic panel

2 SOLAR PANELS

Both solar thermal panels and solar voltaic panels are fitted to the roof of the house on the side that gets the most sun. Most solar panels look the same, but if you see ones made up of tubes, these are definitely solar thermal panels, used to heat water.

Hot water for the bath

Many houses combine solar panels with an ordinary boiler, so you've always got hot water, even when the weather's terrible.

Hot water for the kitchen

3 GETTING PUMPED UP

To make solar thermal energy, the house needs to be fitted with a pump. This pushes a special kind of fluid around a pipe inside your house. The pipe makes a big loop that starts inside your water tank, runs up to the roof, around the solar panels, and then back down to the tank again.

Water tank

Pump pushes fluid through the long loop of pipe

Side of house that gets the most sun

SOLAR POWER STATIONS

You don't just find solar panels on houses. There are also huge solar power stations. These use thousands of mirrors to capture sunlight and reflect it onto a central tower, called a **receiver**. Running through the receiver are pipes full of a special liquid that gets heated by the sunlight and turned into steam. This, in turn, drives a turbine (a kind of big engine) to produce electricity. The electricity travels through overhead or underground cables, and eventually reaches your house.

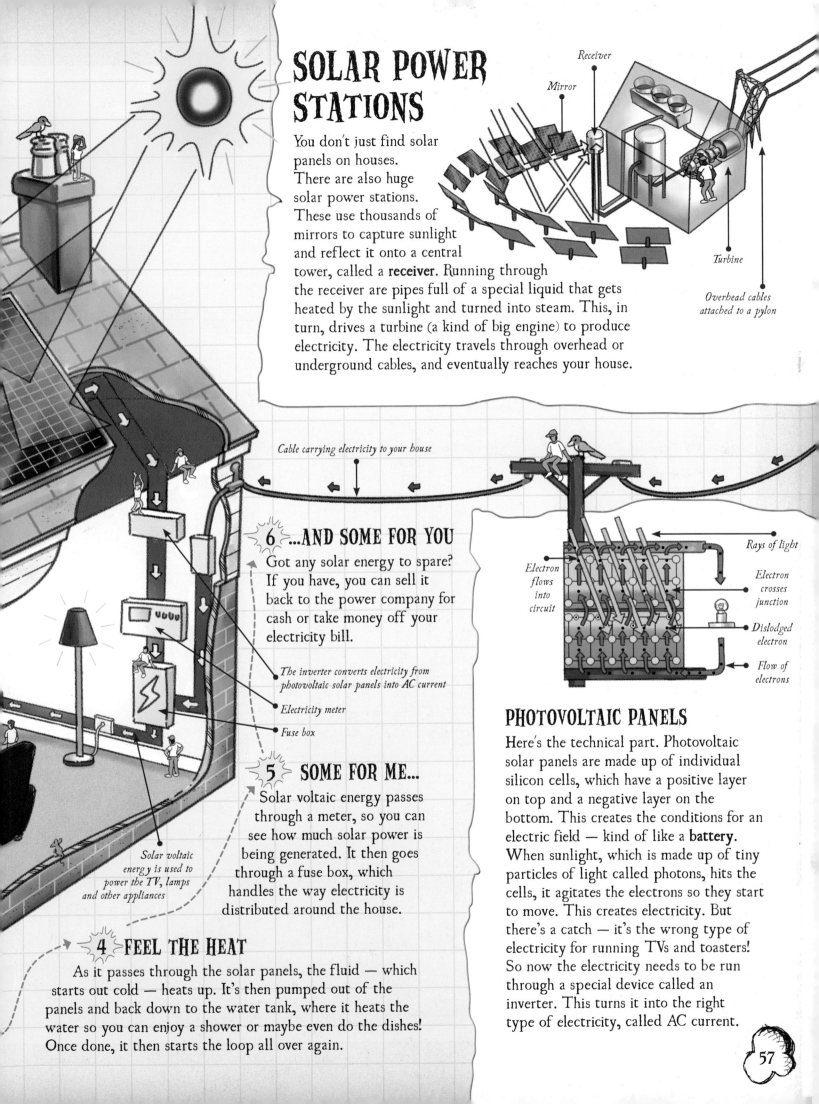

Receiver

Mirror

Turbine

Overhead cables attached to a pylon

Cable carrying electricity to your house

6 ...AND SOME FOR YOU

Got any solar energy to spare? If you have, you can sell it back to the power company for cash or take money off your electricity bill.

The inverter converts electricity from photovoltaic solar panels into AC current

Electricity meter

Fuse box

5 SOME FOR ME...

Solar voltaic energy passes through a meter, so you can see how much solar power is being generated. It then goes through a fuse box, which handles the way electricity is distributed around the house.

Solar voltaic energy is used to power the TV, lamps and other appliances

4 FEEL THE HEAT

As it passes through the solar panels, the fluid — which starts out cold — heats up. It's then pumped out of the panels and back down to the water tank, where it heats the water so you can enjoy a shower or maybe even do the dishes! Once done, it then starts the loop all over again.

Rays of light

Electron flows into circuit

Electron crosses junction

Dislodged electron

Flow of electrons

PHOTOVOLTAIC PANELS

Here's the technical part. Photovoltaic solar panels are made up of individual silicon cells, which have a positive layer on top and a negative layer on the bottom. This creates the conditions for an electric field — kind of like a **battery**. When sunlight, which is made up of tiny particles of light called photons, hits the cells, it agitates the electrons so they start to move. This creates electricity. But there's a catch — it's the wrong type of electricity for running TVs and toasters! So now the electricity needs to be run through a special device called an inverter. This turns it into the right type of electricity, called AC current.

DOORBELL

If you have ever wondered how a doorbell works, here is your chance to find out. Like many machines, it uses electricity. When a finger presses the button, electricity produces a **magnetic field** that pulls a hammer onto a bell, making the bell ring. If the bell only rang once, it wouldn't attract much attention. Luckily, this doorbell is designed to keep clanging as long as the button is depressed. The result is a noise that no one could ignore!

1 PRESS FOR ACTION

When someone rings a doorbell, the button completes a **circuit** and electricity begins to flow.

POWER SOURCE

The doorbell is powered either by its own batteries or by electricity from a power plant.

Switch operated by pressing the doorbell's button

Springs pull movable contact back so it touches nonmoving contact again

CREATING A MAGNETIC FIELD

When electricity passes through a metal wire, a magnetic field forms around the wire. You can see this if you surround a wire with compasses. Normally, compass needles point north, but as soon as electricity flows through the wire, the needles show a magnetic field has been created. The wire now has the qualities of a magnet, and it can **attract** and **repel** metal objects.

Switch

Compasses showing a magnetic field has been created

Compasses all pointing north

Battery

Transformer

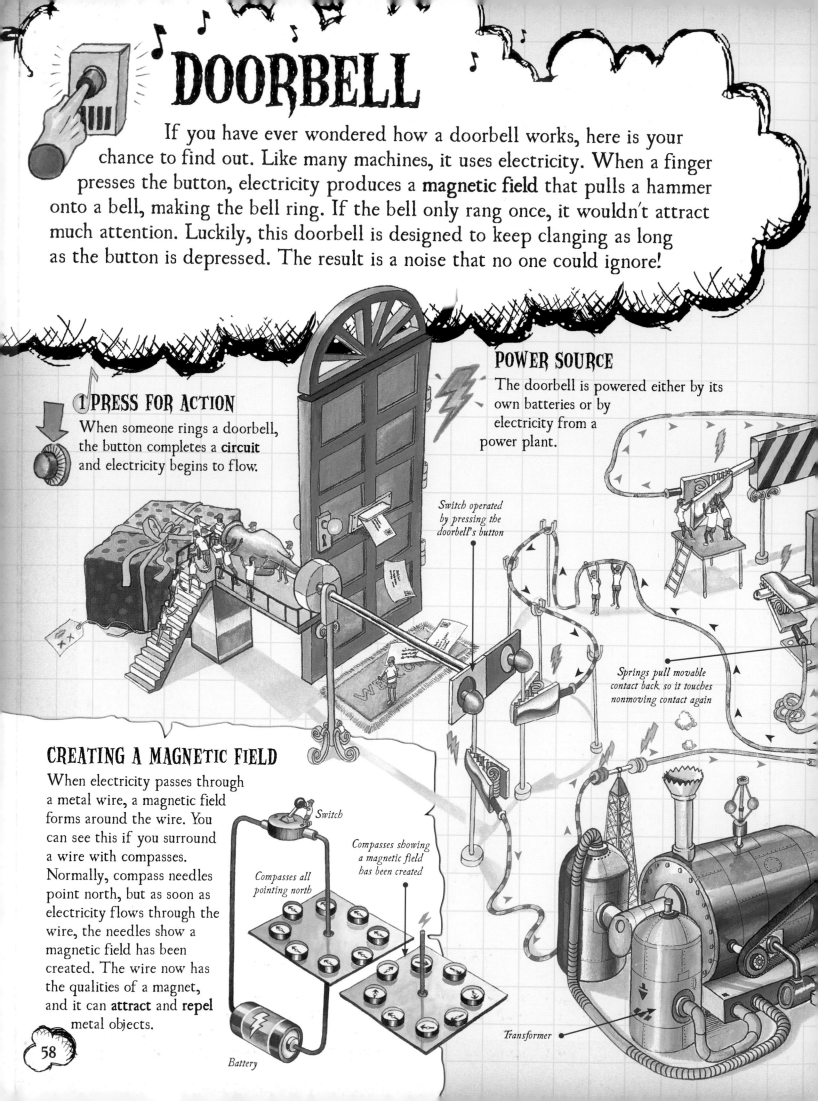

58

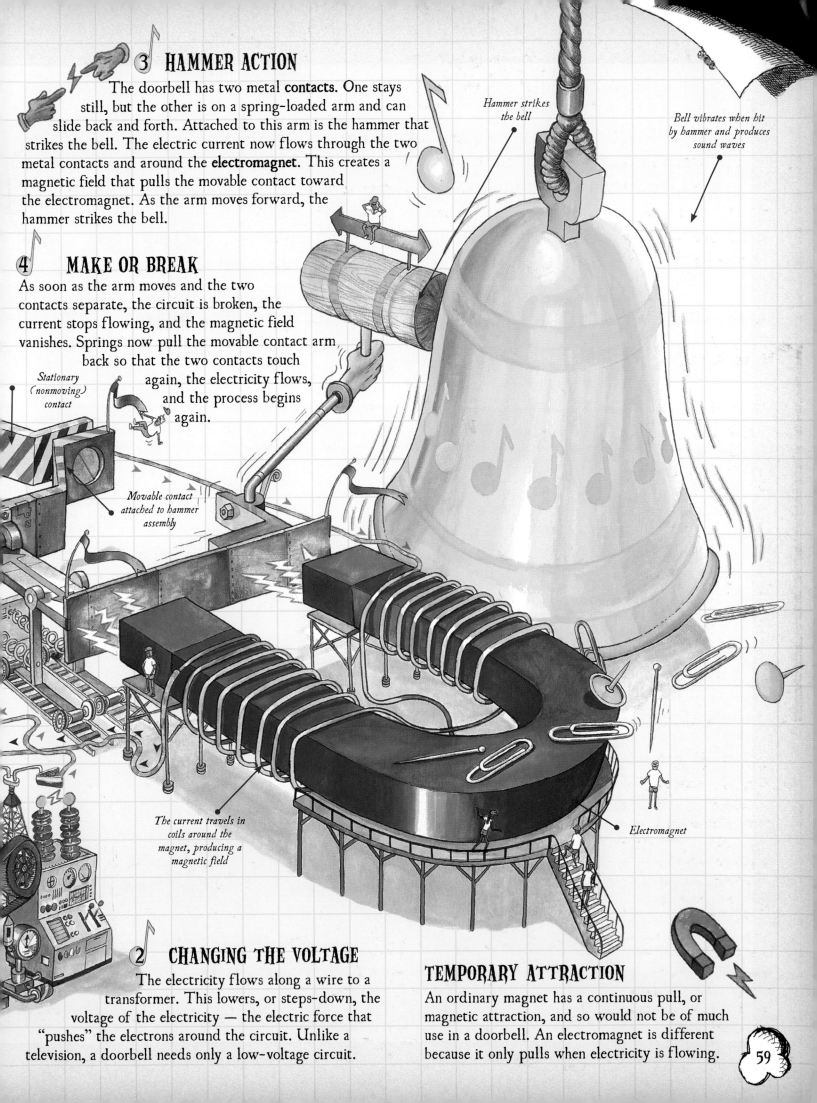

3 HAMMER ACTION

The doorbell has two metal **contacts**. One stays still, but the other is on a spring-loaded arm and can slide back and forth. Attached to this arm is the hammer that strikes the bell. The electric current now flows through the two metal contacts and around the **electromagnet**. This creates a magnetic field that pulls the movable contact toward the electromagnet. As the arm moves forward, the hammer strikes the bell.

4 MAKE OR BREAK

As soon as the arm moves and the two contacts separate, the circuit is broken, the current stops flowing, and the magnetic field vanishes. Springs now pull the movable contact arm back so that the two contacts touch again, the electricity flows, and the process begins again.

Hammer strikes the bell

Bell vibrates when hit by hammer and produces sound waves

Stationary (nonmoving) contact

Movable contact attached to hammer assembly

The current travels in coils around the magnet, producing a magnetic field

Electromagnet

2 CHANGING THE VOLTAGE

The electricity flows along a wire to a transformer. This lowers, or steps-down, the voltage of the electricity — the electric force that "pushes" the electrons around the circuit. Unlike a television, a doorbell needs only a low-voltage circuit.

TEMPORARY ATTRACTION

An ordinary magnet has a continuous pull, or magnetic attraction, and so would not be of much use in a doorbell. An electromagnet is different because it only pulls when electricity is flowing.

59

3-D PRINTER

Instead of having to go to a shop every time you need something — let's say a new mug — imagine you could just call up the basic plans on your computer, make a few changes, and then build the mug yourself. Well, that's exactly what you can do with a 3-D printer.

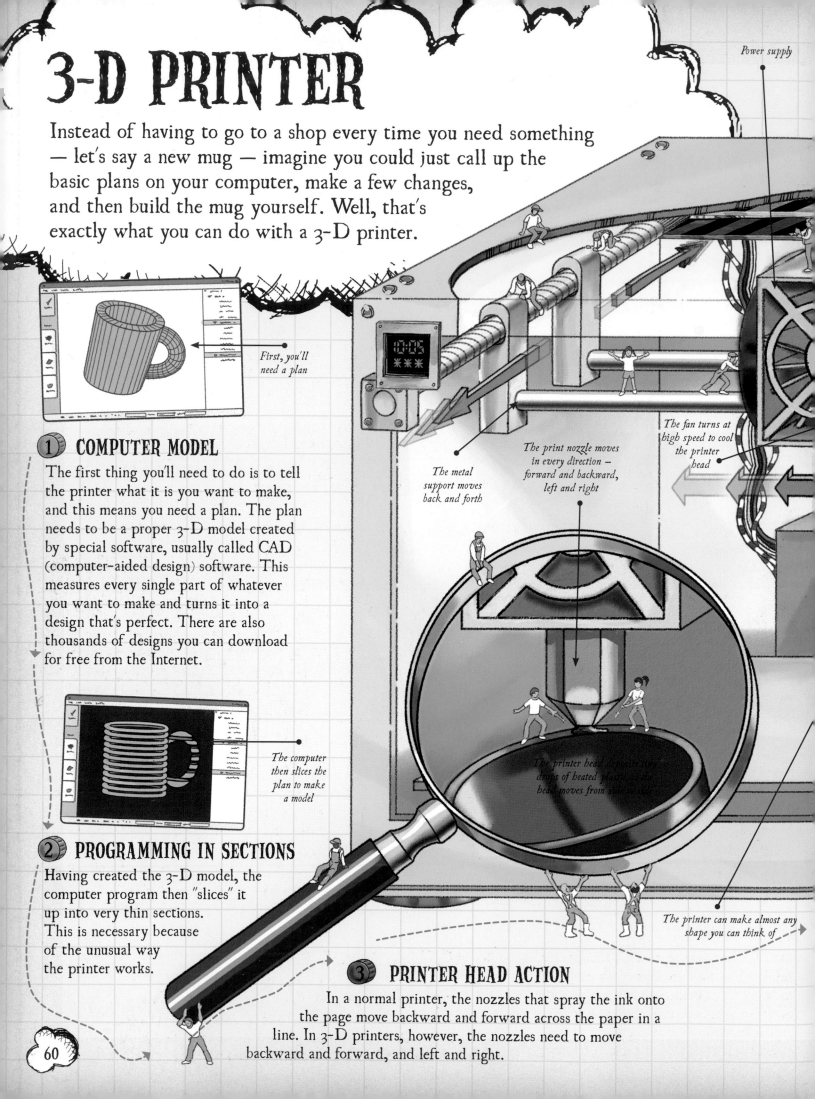

First, you'll need a plan

① COMPUTER MODEL

The first thing you'll need to do is to tell the printer what it is you want to make, and this means you need a plan. The plan needs to be a proper 3-D model created by special software, usually called CAD (computer-aided design) software. This measures every single part of whatever you want to make and turns it into a design that's perfect. There are also thousands of designs you can download for free from the Internet.

The computer then slices the plan to make a model

② PROGRAMMING IN SECTIONS

Having created the 3-D model, the computer program then "slices" it up into very thin sections. This is necessary because of the unusual way the printer works.

③ PRINTER HEAD ACTION

In a normal printer, the nozzles that spray the ink onto the page move backward and forward across the paper in a line. In 3-D printers, however, the nozzles need to move backward and forward, and left and right.

Power supply

The metal support moves back and forth

The print nozzle moves in every direction — forward and backward, left and right

The fan turns at high speed to cool the printer head

The printer head deposits tiny drops of heated plastic as the head moves from side to side

The printer can make almost any shape you can think of

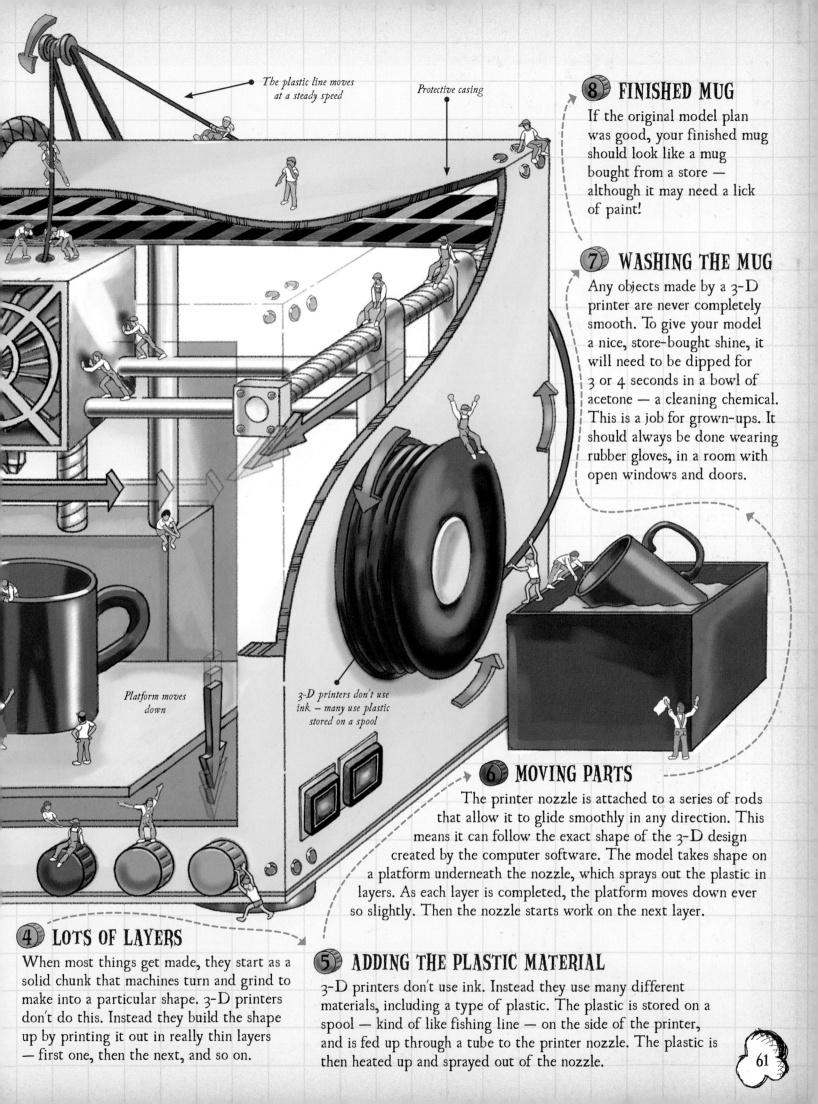

The plastic line moves at a steady speed

Protective casing

8 FINISHED MUG

If the original model plan was good, your finished mug should look like a mug bought from a store — although it may need a lick of paint!

7 WASHING THE MUG

Any objects made by a 3-D printer are never completely smooth. To give your model a nice, store-bought shine, it will need to be dipped for 3 or 4 seconds in a bowl of acetone — a cleaning chemical. This is a job for grown-ups. It should always be done wearing rubber gloves, in a room with open windows and doors.

Platform moves down

3-D printers don't use ink — many use plastic stored on a spool

6 MOVING PARTS

The printer nozzle is attached to a series of rods that allow it to glide smoothly in any direction. This means it can follow the exact shape of the 3-D design created by the computer software. The model takes shape on a platform underneath the nozzle, which sprays out the plastic in layers. As each layer is completed, the platform moves down ever so slightly. Then the nozzle starts work on the next layer.

4 LOTS OF LAYERS

When most things get made, they start as a solid chunk that machines turn and grind to make into a particular shape. 3-D printers don't do this. Instead they build the shape up by printing it out in really thin layers — first one, then the next, and so on.

5 ADDING THE PLASTIC MATERIAL

3-D printers don't use ink. Instead they use many different materials, including a type of plastic. The plastic is stored on a spool — kind of like fishing line — on the side of the printer, and is fed up through a tube to the printer nozzle. The plastic is then heated up and sprayed out of the nozzle.

WEATHER REPORT

If you want to know if it will be sunny or rainy tomorrow, you can watch the weather report on TV. But how do weather forecasters know what the weather will be like? They find out by watching the weather all around the world and then predicting how it will develop and change over the next few days.

Clouds are made from tiny drops of water that may fall as rain

How rainy is it?

How windy is it?

How damp is it?

How warm is it?

Weather balloon

Radio transmitter

Weather station

Weather office

② IN THE AIR

Weather forecasters need to know what is going on high up in the sky as well as at ground level. Every day, hundreds of weather balloons soar up to 20 miles into the sky. They carry instruments that measure the weather conditions and automatically transmit the results back to base.

① WEATHER WATCHING

All around the world, weather stations measure how damp the air is, how dense it is (the air pressure), how warm it is, how much rain falls, and the speed of the wind. The stations send their findings by radio to a local weather office. The weather office gathers the information, or data, from balloons, **satellites**, and local weather stations, and beams this information up to another satellite.

Global telecommunications satellite

Weather center receives data

4 ARE YOU RECEIVING ME?

A global telecommunications satellite (GTS) receives data from all over the world and beams it back down to a main weather center. There, the data is fed into a powerful computer called a supercomputer. The computer prints out exactly what it thinks the next measurements will be at each weather station.

Computer printout

3 VIEW FROM SPACE

Satellites circling Earth in space take pictures of the world below. They transmit the pictures back to a weather office on the ground. The pictures show forecasters where the clouds are and what weather patterns are developing.

5 WEATHER CHART

Next, the computer uses the data to make a chart showing what the weather will be like in each area.

The computer's predictions are sent out to all the weather offices and stations

Making the weather chart

Radio waves

The weather forecaster explains the weather map

Weather map

Watching the TV weather report

6 TOMORROW'S WEATHER

For the TV weather report, the forecasters use the weather chart to make up a map we can all understand. Little suns mean a sunny day, clouds represent overcast skies, droplets indicate rain, and so on. Now you know whether to wear a heavy coat or shorts tomorrow!

TELEVISION

How can you visit Mars, follow your favorite games, and watch wildlife without even getting out of your chair? By watching television, of course! But what is the secret of television?

Camera

Mic

Studio

1 THE PICTURE

When a TV camera takes pictures of a scene, rows of tiny **photo cells** inside the camera change the pictures into electrical blips.

Picture signal

Cameras record in just three colors: red, green, and blue

2 LISTEN UP

A **microphone**, or mic, records the sound. The sound, like the pictures, is recorded as a pattern of electrical blips.

3 LIVE OR RECORDED?

News reports and sports events are often sent out "live" as they happen. Dramas are usually recorded and sent out later.

4 FROM BLIPS TO RIPPLES

The picture and sound signals are sent to a TV **transmitter**. Strong magnets turn the electrical blips in the signals into invisible ripples of energy called radio waves.

5 BROADCASTING

Sending out TV pictures and sound is called broadcasting. The radio waves spread out from the transmitter into the air. TV programs can also be sent as electrical blips straight to your home through cables.

Changing the signals to radio waves

7 PICKING UP THE VIBES

An antenna picks up signals beamed straight from the TV station. TV signals bounced off satellites in space are picked up by a dish-shaped receiver.

6 TV FROM SPACE

Sometimes TV programs have to be broadcast over a large area or to faraway places — even to the other side of the world. When this happens, the TV signal has to be bounced off a communications satellite orbiting Earth high up in space.

Radio wave

8 BLIPS AGAIN

The dish and aerial change the radio waves back into electrical blips. These go to your TV set.

9 WHAT A SHOW!

A **loudspeaker** in the TV set reproduces the sound. Special electron guns at the back of the set fire rays at the screen and make it glow with tiny dots of blue, green, and red. From a distance, these give the illusion of a full-color picture.

ROCKET LAUNCH

It's not easy getting a satellite into space. You need a lot of rocket power to get anything off the ground, whether it's only going into low Earth **orbit** (anything higher than 100 miles) or much further. And remember, it's not just the weight of the satellite that needs to be lifted, it's also the weight of the massive rocket you're using to carry the satellite, and the weight of the fuel you'll need!

 1 ENGINES

Most engines rotate, but rocket engines are different — they are reaction engines. Imagine you were standing on a skateboard holding a fire fighter's hose that was spraying a strong jet of water. The action of the water flying out of the hose would push the skateboard along in the other direction (this is the reaction). It can take several fire fighters to hold a hose because the reaction is so strong! That's how rocket engines work — except they use rocket fuel, not water.

Booster engine

*Less than 1 minute later, the booster engines cut out and the booster package is **jettisoned***

Solid rocket boosters

Both pairs of solid rocket boosters use up their fuel during the first 2 minutes of flight before being jettisoned

ROCKET THRUST

Jet engines work by mixing oxygen and fuel together, and then igniting them to produce **thrust**. However, because there's no air in space, rockets have to carry their own oxygen with them in liquid form in a huge tank.

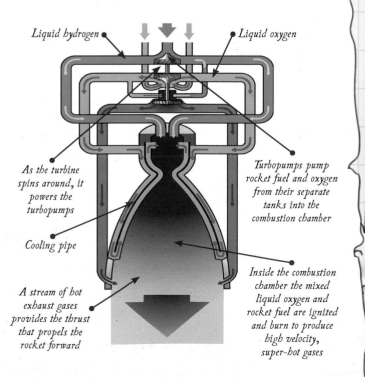

Liquid hydrogen

Liquid oxygen

As the turbine spins around, it powers the turbopumps

Cooling pipe

A stream of hot exhaust gases provides the thrust that propels the rocket forward

Turbopumps pump rocket fuel and oxygen from their separate tanks into the combustion chamber

Inside the combustion chamber the mixed liquid oxygen and rocket fuel are ignited and burn to produce high velocity, super-hot gases

2 LAUNCHING THE ROCKET

Most rockets are sent into space from a launchpad. This giant frame serves two purposes. First, it allows engineers and technicians to fill the rocket with fuel and check the outside for any problems. Second, rockets need support until they're ready for lift off. They are secured to the frame by special bolts that have a tiny explosive charge in them. When the rocket is ready to launch, these charges are set off, the bolts break, and up goes the rocket.

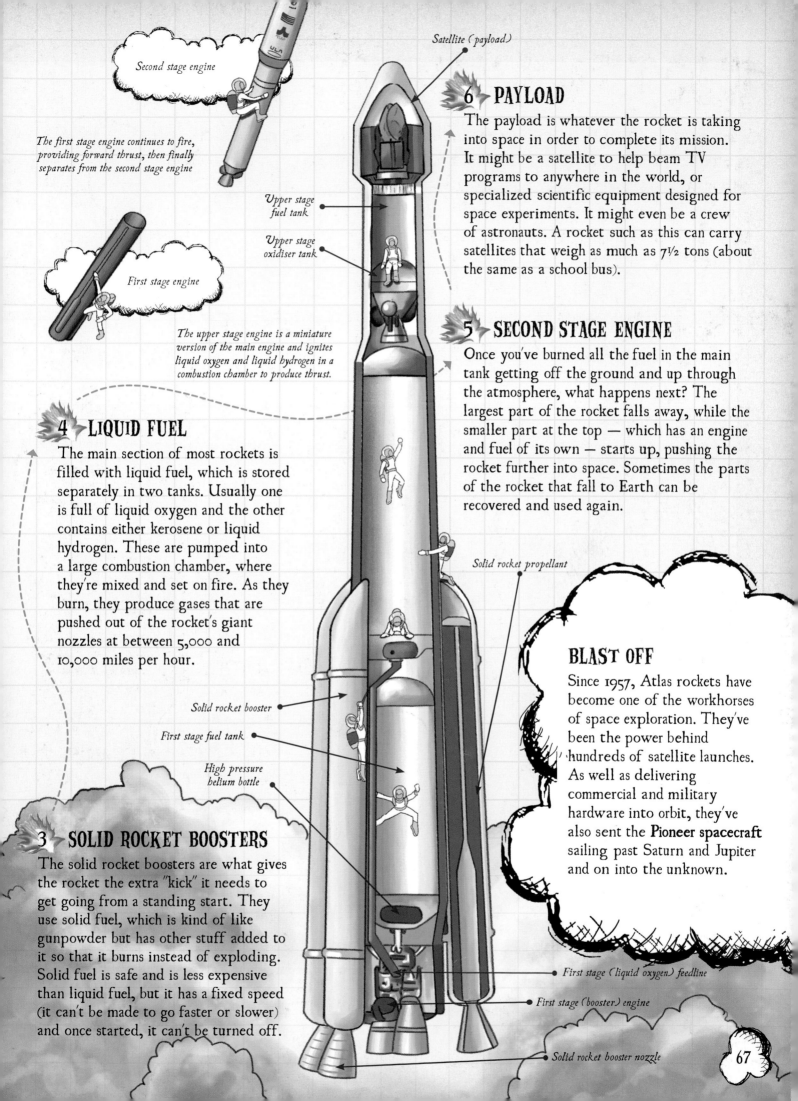

Second stage engine

The first stage engine continues to fire, providing forward thrust, then finally separates from the second stage engine

First stage engine

The upper stage engine is a miniature version of the main engine and ignites liquid oxygen and liquid hydrogen in a combustion chamber to produce thrust.

Satellite (payload)

Upper stage fuel tank

Upper stage oxidiser tank

6 ▸ PAYLOAD

The payload is whatever the rocket is taking into space in order to complete its mission. It might be a satellite to help beam TV programs to anywhere in the world, or specialized scientific equipment designed for space experiments. It might even be a crew of astronauts. A rocket such as this can carry satellites that weigh as much as 7½ tons (about the same as a school bus).

5 ▸ SECOND STAGE ENGINE

Once you've burned all the fuel in the main tank getting off the ground and up through the atmosphere, what happens next? The largest part of the rocket falls away, while the smaller part at the top — which has an engine and fuel of its own — starts up, pushing the rocket further into space. Sometimes the parts of the rocket that fall to Earth can be recovered and used again.

4 ▸ LIQUID FUEL

The main section of most rockets is filled with liquid fuel, which is stored separately in two tanks. Usually one is full of liquid oxygen and the other contains either kerosene or liquid hydrogen. These are pumped into a large combustion chamber, where they're mixed and set on fire. As they burn, they produce gases that are pushed out of the rocket's giant nozzles at between 5,000 and 10,000 miles per hour.

Solid rocket propellant

BLAST OFF

Since 1957, Atlas rockets have become one of the workhorses of space exploration. They've been the power behind hundreds of satellite launches. As well as delivering commercial and military hardware into orbit, they've also sent the **Pioneer spacecraft** sailing past Saturn and Jupiter and on into the unknown.

Solid rocket booster

First stage fuel tank

High pressure helium bottle

3 ▸ SOLID ROCKET BOOSTERS

The solid rocket boosters are what gives the rocket the extra "kick" it needs to get going from a standing start. They use solid fuel, which is kind of like gunpowder but has other stuff added to it so that it burns instead of exploding. Solid fuel is safe and is less expensive than liquid fuel, but it has a fixed speed (it can't be made to go faster or slower) and once started, it can't be turned off.

First stage (liquid oxygen) feedline

First stage (booster) engine

Solid rocket booster nozzle

AUTOMOBILE

You probably see hundreds of cars every single day — there are more than one billion in the world — but have you ever stopped to think about how they work and the technology used inside them? Here we reveal the insides of one of the most popular, and best loved, machines of all time.

1 FOUR CYLINDER ENGINE

A car engine needs air and fuel to work. Mixing the two in a small space and adding a spark produces enough energy to move four sets of pistons up and down. These pistons are attached to a pole called a crank shaft, which in turn drives a much longer prop (propeller) shaft that runs through the middle of the car. As the pistons go up and down, they turn the prop shaft.

2 PROP SHAFT AND DIFFERENTIAL

The prop shaft needs to be able to turn the rear **axle**. It does this using a fancy gearing device. This device, called the differential, is also able to turn the back wheels at different speeds, so the car can go around the corners smoothly.

3 GEARBOX

The gearbox does two things. Its first job is to connect and disconnect the engine and the wheels, so you can sit in traffic without the car moving. Second, there's a limit to the number of times a car engine can turn the crank shaft in a minute, so the **gears** are used to control this and strike the right balance between the number of times the engine turns and the speed you want the car to go. In a standard car, the gearbox is controlled by a gear stick and a pedal called a clutch. To break the connection between the engine and the wheels, you push down the clutch with your foot. Then you change gear and release the pedal, and the car will use the new gear.

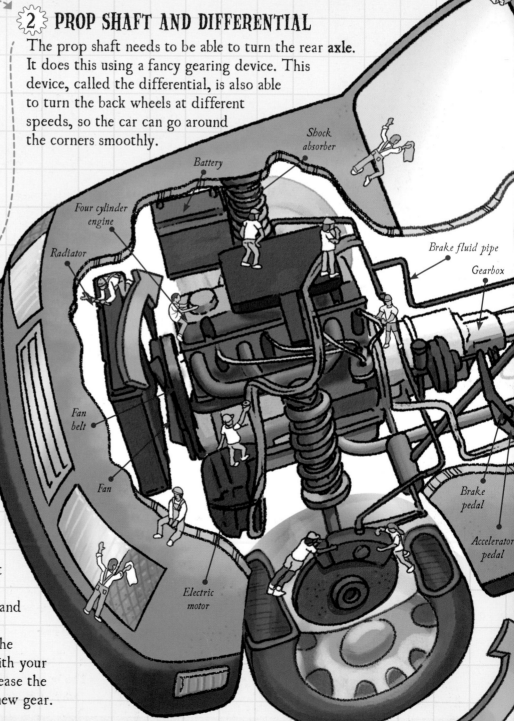

Four cylinder engine

Radiator

Battery

Shock absorber

Brake fluid pipe

Gearbox

Fan belt

Fan

Electric motor

Brake pedal

Accelerator pedal

72

4 FUEL TANK

When you fill up with fuel, the fuel goes into a tank, and from there it's pumped to the engine. In some vehicles the pump is at the front of the car and is powered by the engine. In others it's inside the fuel tank, and runs off the car battery.

5 HYBRID BATTERY

Some modern cars use both an ordinary engine and an electric motor. The electric motor sits between the engine and the hybrid battery, and it converts some of the energy produced by the engine into electricity, which is stored in the hybrid battery. When you brake, the electric motor runs backward, which not only slows the car but also generates even more electricity.

6 EXHAUST AND CATALYTIC CONVERTER

A series of pipes runs from the engine all the way to the back of the car. It takes all the gross gases from the engine and runs them through a catalytic converter — a box coated with chemicals. This helps to remove some of the harmful gases, such as carbon monoxide, before shooting them out of the exhaust pipe.

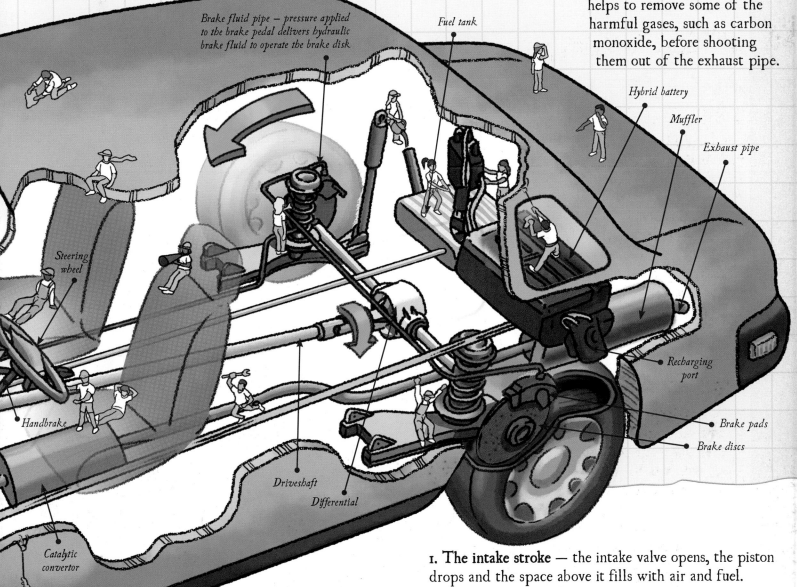

Brake fluid pipe — pressure applied to the brake pedal delivers hydraulic brake fluid to operate the brake disk

Fuel tank

Hybrid battery

Muffler

Exhaust pipe

Steering wheel

Recharging port

Handbrake

Brake pads

Brake discs

Driveshaft

Differential

Catalytic convertor

FOUR STROKE CYCLE

A car engine runs by letting off hundreds of tiny explosions every minute in what's called the four stroke cycle. Here's how it works.

(1)   (2)   (3)   (4)

1. The intake stroke — the intake valve opens, the piston drops and the space above it fills with air and fuel.

2. The compression stroke — the intake valve closes so the air can't escape and the piston moves back up, squeezing the air and fuel mixture.

3. The combustion stroke — a spark lights the mixture to make a little explosion, which forces the piston back down.

4. The exhaust stroke — as the piston reaches the bottom, the outlet valve opens and the gases leftover after the explosion leave the chamber. The piston moves back to the top, and the whole thing starts again.

JET PLANE

A fully loaded jet plane such as this one weighs about 54,000 pounds. So how do you get all that weight up in the air safely and then make it go where you want it to go?

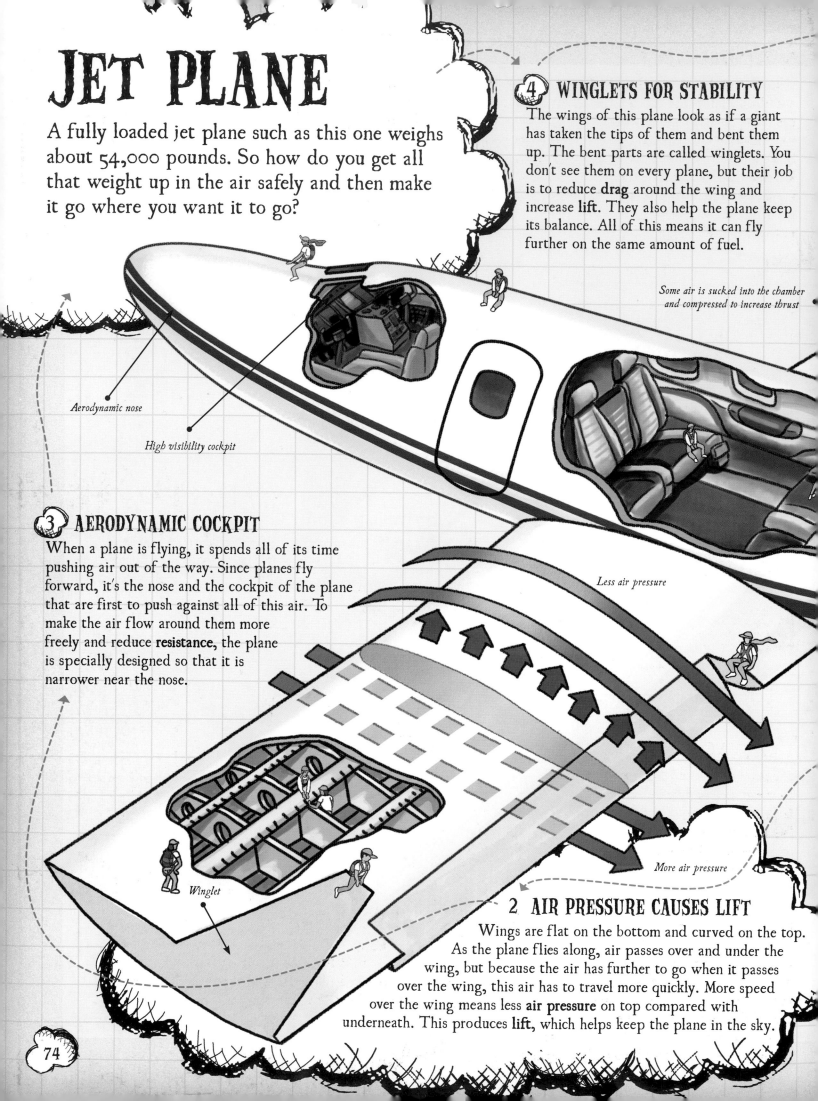

Aerodynamic nose

High visibility cockpit

4 WINGLETS FOR STABILITY

The wings of this plane look as if a giant has taken the tips of them and bent them up. The bent parts are called winglets. You don't see them on every plane, but their job is to reduce **drag** around the wing and increase **lift**. They also help the plane keep its balance. All of this means it can fly further on the same amount of fuel.

Some air is sucked into the chamber and compressed to increase thrust

Less air pressure

3 AERODYNAMIC COCKPIT

When a plane is flying, it spends all of its time pushing air out of the way. Since planes fly forward, it's the nose and the cockpit of the plane that are first to push against all of this air. To make the air flow around them more freely and reduce **resistance**, the plane is specially designed so that it is narrower near the nose.

Winglet

More air pressure

2 AIR PRESSURE CAUSES LIFT

Wings are flat on the bottom and curved on the top. As the plane flies along, air passes over and under the wing, but because the air has further to go when it passes over the wing, this air has to travel more quickly. More speed over the wing means less **air pressure** on top compared with underneath. This produces **lift**, which helps keep the plane in the sky.

74

5 FLAPS ON WINGS

Once in the air, you need to be able to steer the plane left and right, and up and down. Pilots use the controls in the cockpit to move the various flaps on each wing; when the pilot turns the controls to the left, the flap on the left wing goes up and the one on the right wing goes down. Since a raised flap reduces lift and a lowered flap increases it, the plane will start to roll to the left and then turn in that direction.

To ascend, pull back on the stick to raise the tail flap. Tail goes down, nose goes up.

To start turning, roll the plane in the direction you want to go — in this case to the left.

To descend, push forward on the stick to lower the tail flap. Tail goes up, nose goes down.

Some air is sucked in and bypasses the combustion chamber

Tail rudder

Combustion chamber

Fan

Stationary blades make the engine more efficient

Cool air bypasses engine and makes up three quarters of the total thrust.

*Turbines drive the front fan and internal **compressors***

Driveshaft

Hot gases turn the turbines and are then pushed out the back of the engine

1 JET ENGINE

Air gets sucked into the front of the engine by a series of large fans. Some of this air bypasses the main workings and goes straight out of the back of the engine. The remainder is compressed to increase its **pressure,** and then mixed with jet fuel in a part of the engine called a combustion chamber. Add a spark, and when the mixture catches light it expands and shoots out of the back, pushing the plane forward. This type is called a turbofan engine, and is much quieter than other kinds of jet engines.

6 TAIL RUDDER

Unlike a boat, the rudder on a jet plane isn't used to steer it. Instead, it's used to prevent the plane from swinging left and right while it travels in a straight line. This movement is called yaw.

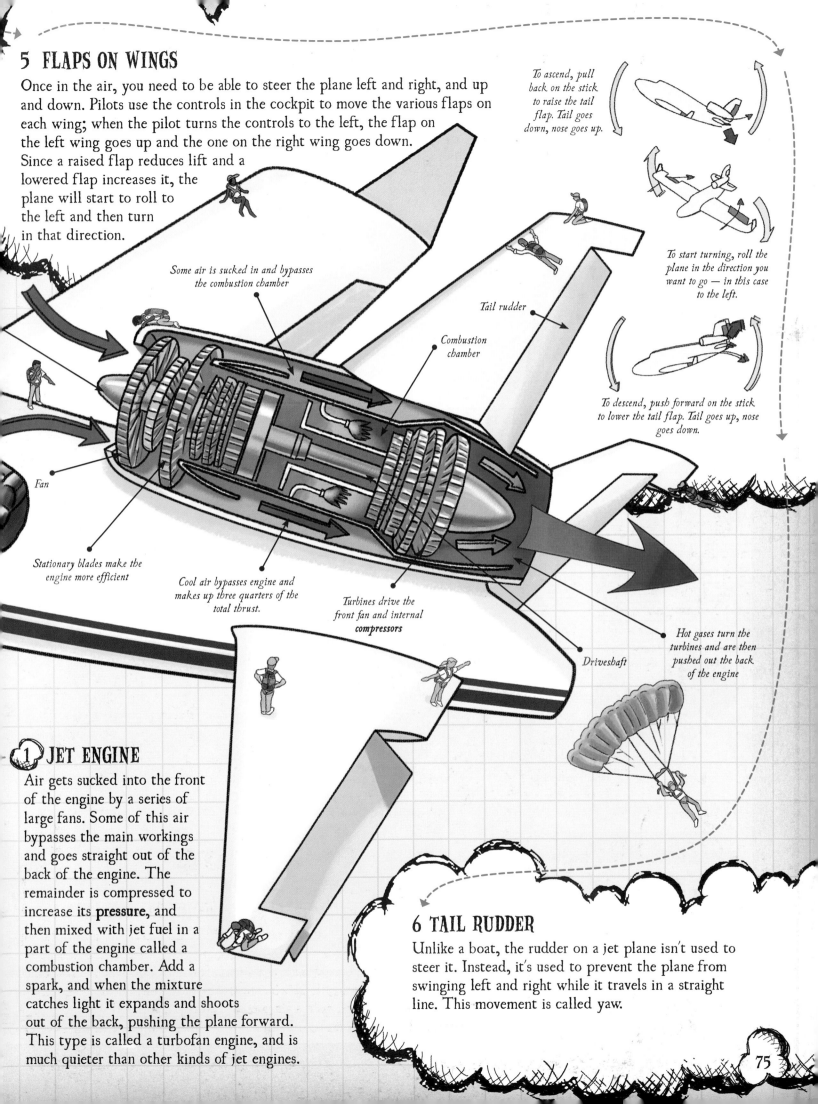

GLOSSARY

air pressure How thick or dense the air is. High-pressure air is thick; low-pressure air is thin.

app Short for "application," an app is a small program that runs on a smartphone or tablet.

atoms The smallest complete particles of any solid, liquid, or gas. Atoms make up everything, from the air we breathe to the machines we use.

attract To pull something without actually touching it.

axle A rotating rod. Axles are used to turn wheels or to carry movement from one place to another.

bacteria Tiny living cells. "Good" bacteria help us in all kinds of ways, but "bad" bacteria, or germs, can make us very sick.

battery A cell that stores electricity by turning it into chemical energy.

bearing A part of a machine that reduces friction. Bearings separate moving surfaces, and they roll, so one surface can slide past another.

cam A device shaped like a lopsided wheel that changes rotary (around and around) movement into up-and-down movement. A cam is mounted on a rotating shaft.

cellular network A cell phone or wireless network that divides an area of land into sections or "cells." Each cell has a base station, used for connecting cell phones to the telephone network.

circuit A loop that has no open ends. Electrical circuits can be very short or many miles long.

compressor A device that squeezes (compresses) a liquid or a gas, forcing it into a small space.

condense To turn from a gas or a vapor into a liquid. Gases and vapors condense either when they are cooled, or when they are compressed.

contact (electrical) Something that is designed to complete a circuit so that electricity can flow. Most electrical contacts are made of metal.

current (electric) A stream of moving particles, called electrons, that carry energy. When an electric current is switched on, energy can travel a huge distance almost instantly.

drag The force that planes push against so they can move forward. Drag is why planes need engines.

electricity A form of energy that is carried through wires.

electromagnet A magnet that works because of electricity. Unlike permanent magnets, electromagnets only work when electricity flows through them.

electron A tiny particle that carries a negative electric charge. Electrons linked together make up an electrical current. All atoms contain electrons.

enzyme A substance that speeds up a chemical reaction thousands or millions of times.

evaporate To turn into a vapor. Water slowly evaporates if it's left in a dry place.

ferment The process by which yeast helps sugar split into alcohol and carbon dioxide gas.

filter bed Layers of sand and small stones covered by bacteria that clean dirty water trickling through them.

flocs Clumps of dirt that form when water is cleaned.

friction A force that slows down a moving object. Friction can be reduced by using oil or bearings, but it can never be stopped altogether.

fuse A safety device that stops an electric current from flowing if too much electricity is being used.

gear A toothed wheel designed to transfer movement. Gears turn each other by their interlocking teeth, and they can be used to change a movement's speed, force, or direction.

generator A machine that makes an electric current using a coil of copper wire spinning between the poles of a large magnet.

GPS satellites About 30 Global Positioning Satellites go around the Earth "pinging" billions of devices, such as phones and car satellite navigation (satnav) systems, so you know exactly where you are.

hydroelectric station Place where electricity is made when a generator is turned by the force of moving water.

icon A little picture on a computer or smartphone screen that represents an app or other program, an option (choice), or a window.

incinerator A very hot oven where trash is burned.

insulating Blocking the path of heat or electricity. Plastics, glass, ceramics, and rubber are insulating materials.

ionized Made up by ions. Ions are atoms that have gained or lost electrons. Unlike atoms, they have an electrical charge.

jettisoned Deliberately dropped from an aircraft or spacecraft in flight.

lift The upward force that keeps an aircraft in the air. Lift is created by differences in air pressure.

loudspeaker A device that changes an electric current into sound.

magnet A piece of metal (usually steel) that pulls other metals toward it or pushes them away with an invisible force called magnetism. Magnets can also move electrons through metal wires.

magnetic field An invisible region around a magnet in which its effects can be felt. The field is strongest in the area closest to the magnet.

mains Underground pipes or cables that carry water, electricity, or gas to your home.

meter A device that measures how much water, gas, or electricity you use.

microphone A device that changes the vibrations of sound (such as voice) into an electric current.

microprocessor An electronic device that carries out calculations. Microprocessors are at the heart of all computers and calculators.

microwaves Tiny pulses of energy that can carry a phone call to a satellite and back, or heat up a meal.

molecule A chemical unit, such as water, which is made up of two or more atoms that are linked together.

nozzle A funnel-shaped opening, narrow end pointing outward, at the end of a pipe or tube. A liquid or gas speeds up when it passes through a nozzle, and expands when it leaves it.

nuclear fuel Fuel, such as uranium, that can be used in nuclear reactors as a source of electricity.

operating system An electronic "conductor" that makes sure all the parts of a computer — hardware and software — work together in harmony.

optical character reader An electronic computer eye that can read both letters and numbers.

orbit The curved path a spacecraft takes around a planet or moon.

photo cell A device that changes the light coming into a TV camera into electrical blips.

Pioneer spacecraft A series of American robot spacecraft sent to observe the Sun, Jupiter, Saturn, and Venus. Pioneer 10 is now more than 7 billion miles from Earth.

postal code A code for a street used by computer sorting systems.

pressure The force with which things press against their surroundings. The pressure of a gas or vapor can be increased by heating it up.

radiation A form of energy that spreads out from an object. Light is a form of radiation.

radioactive Giving off radiation. Some radioactive substances are dangerous because their radiation can harm living things.

radio waves Invisible pulses of energy that spread TV or radio signals through the air.

receiver A device that picks up incoming signals. Televisions, radios, and telephones all have receivers.

recycled Waste materials that have been used to make new things.

repel To push something away without actually touching it. Magnets repel each other if their matching poles are lined up.

reservoir A natural or artificial lake or pond, or an underground cavern, used for storing water.

resistance An opposing force.

satellite A pilotless spacecraft that circles, or orbits, the Earth.

sedimentation tank A container in which dirty water is left to stand so lumps of dirt can sink to the bottom.

sewer A huge drain for waste water and sewage.

sizing machine A machine that sorts letters according to their size.

sludge The mud that settles out of sewage or dirty water.

sludge digestion tank A container in which bacteria eat the sludge removed from sewage.

sound wave Waves of pressure that carry sound. Both in ears and microphones, these waves are converted into movement.

stream A continous flow of music or video received over the Internet.

suction Removing air from a space in order to force a liquid (or, in the case of a vacuum cleaner, different air) into that space.

threshing A process that shakes out the grains from harvested wheat.

thrust The force that moves an aircraft through the air. Engines produce thrust.

touchscreen A screen on a smartphone or tablet that allows you to choose things, or change the size of pictures, just by touching the screen.

transformer A device that makes an electric current stronger or weaker.

transmitter A device that sends out TV, radio, or telephone signals.

transponder Electrical device on a satellite designed to receive a specific signal and automatically transmit a specific reply.

turbine A special wheel with slanting blades. Wind, water, or steam rushes past the turbine and pushes on the blades. This spins the wheel so that it drives a generator.

valve A device that lets something flow in one direction, but not in another. Valves are often found in machines that pump liquids or gases.

vapor A gas that has been formed by the evaporation of a liquid.

winnowing Separating wheat grains from their husks.